SHEARER WONDERLAND

SHEARER WONDERLAND

DUNCAN SHEARER

WITH PAUL SMITH

BLACK & WHITE PUBLISHING

First published 2010
by Black & White Publishing Ltd
29 Ocean Drive, Edinburgh EH6 6JL

3 5 7 9 10 8 6 4 2   10 11 12

ISBN: 978 1 84502 316 4

Typeset by Ellipsis Books Limited, Glasgow
Printed and bound by MPG Books Ltd, Bodmin

CONTENTS

1	A SENSE OF PERSPECTIVE	1
2	TRIALS AND TRIBULATIONS	9
3	THE JOURNEY BEGINS	15
4	JOINING THE CHELSEA SET	22
5	FROM CITY TO TOWN	37
6	SUSPICIOUS MINDS	44
7	OUT WITH THE OLD, IN WITH THE NEW	54
8	FROM PENALTY BOX TO WITNESS BOX	62
9	LANCASHIRE HOT SHOT	70
10	THIRD TIME LUCKY	83
11	LIKE FATHER, LIKE SON	88
12	ABERDEEN AMBITION	98
13	PRIDE OF SCOTLAND	111
14	THE ROAD TO WEMBLEY	119
15	THE END OF AN ERA	134
16	FOOTBALL'S GREAT DIVIDE	149
17	HAMPDEN GLORY	156
18	HIGHLAND HOMECOMING	167
19	POACHER TURNED GAMEKEEPER	171
20	THE MANAGER, THE DEMONS AND ME	181
21	GOING HOME	187
22	INTO THE RED	194
23	THE BIG CRASH	204
24	LIVING ON BORROWED TIME	213
25	BEGINNING OF THE END	221
26	JOB-SEEKING	228
27	TWO JAGS	234
28	THE FINAL CHAPTER	241

To mum, dad and my big brother Willie

ACKNOWLEDGEMENTS

The first people I should thank are those this book is dedicated to who sadly will not get the chance to read it. To my late mum, dad and brother Willie, I say I love you and miss you. Mum, nobody could make scones like you. Dad, I miss your poaching and shinty stories over a few drams. Willie, sorry you ended up supporting Rangers – but we can carry on that argument another time. They were all there at the beginning of the journey, a road on which so many other people, far too many to mention, have helped me along the way.

Two of the great inspirations have been my children, Hayley and William. I'm proud to be your dad – now stop reading this, and go and clear up your rooms. I have to thank the rest of the Shearer family too, not least my brothers and sisters, for always being there whenever I have needed them.

Mike and Nita, my father- and mother-in-law, have also been a tremendous influence on me since the day they took me under their wing when I moved to London as a young man. I thank them both for their daughter Michele, who became my wife, and Nita for the 'piece of cheese' that was served up for my first meal in England all those years ago.

In football, I must note my appreciation for the late Rod Clyne. It was Rod who spotted my potential while I was playing in the

Highland League, and he and Ian McNeill were brave enough to take a chance on a twenty-one-year-old from the Highlands and take me to Chelsea. I'll be forever grateful that they gave me the opportunity, just as I will always be thankful that John Dennison, Dougie Masson and John Flannigan did their bit to keep me on the straight and narrow when I was a boy starting out in the game with Clach. David McGinlay is another person in the game I must thank for his friendship over the years and for the endless phone calls to keep my spirits up when I was hurting following my sacking by Aberdeen. To hear an old Fort William voice at that time was just what I needed.

I must also thank Paul Smith for all his efforts in working with me to make this book a reality, and to all the team at Black & White Publishing for their enthusiasm and attention to detail. It has been a wonderful project to work on, a real pleasure.

Last, but most importantly, I must thank my wife and best friend Michele. I would never have achieved my football or life dream without you. You have given me constant support – and two great kids that we can both be proud of.

Love you always,

Big D.

XXX

XX

X

1

A SENSE OF PERSPECTIVE

I know many people who would agree with Bill Shankly's famous old claim that football is far more important than life or death. I'm afraid, on that issue at least, the great man got it wrong. Football can give you shiny medals, a big pay packet, a nice house and fancy cars. That's all well and good, but none of that really matters in the grand scheme of things.

It took the death of my brother, William, in 2005 to hammer that home to me. It was a lesson late in life but it is one that will stay with me for the rest of my days. I count myself very fortunate that I managed to get a few seconds with Willie during his final hours and in that time he put life in perspective for me.

I was still coming to terms with everything that had happened when Steve Paterson and I had been in charge at Aberdeen and the way that had come to an end so suddenly. To be part of the management team at Pittodrie had been a dream come true for me and when it was snatched away it hit me hard.

Fortunately I had my big brother to put me in my place. He was terribly ill in hospital, fighting for every breath, when he turned to me and said: 'If you think you're feeling down, try landing up in a wheelchair when you're nineteen. Try getting cancer when you're forty-four. You've nothing to be down about.'

He was right, and I'll never ever forget that. It took something so awful to make me see sense but I'm a better person for it. People often say to me: 'You must be desperate to get back into management.' The truth is all of that is not the be all and end all for me. I'm settled and happy with my wife and have two fit and healthy kids – that is what is important to me, more than anything else in the world. I know where my priorities lie and I feel at peace with myself because of that. I'll never lose the competitive spirit and ambition that I have always had, but now I feel very much that what will be will be. If and when the right opportunity comes my way I'll grab it with both hands, but until then I'm quite content. Any time that I feel myself getting even a little bit down, I think back to that conversation with Willie and snap out of it in an instant. He will always be there with me in spirit.

In so many ways Willie has had a big influence on the decisions I have taken and the path I have followed. That can be traced right back to the start of my career as a professional football player early in 1983, when I signed my first contract with Chelsea. While I was starting off a new life in London, back home in Fort William my big brother was facing far bigger challenges.

I went down to England at a very difficult time for the Shearer family. Just a few weeks earlier William had been involved in a terrible accident. He was nineteen at the time, and had been out at a nightclub in Fort William when he hailed a taxi to take him home. Five minutes into the journey he realised he'd come away without one of his mates and asked the driver to head back and pick him up. To this day we don't know exactly what happened next but from what we can gather the driver tried to turn too quickly, and lost control. The back of the car whipped round and clattered into railings down by the waterfront. Willie was badly injured and was rushed to the local hospital before they realised they were out of their depth and a helicopter was scrambled to take him to a specialist unit down in Edinburgh.

The first anyone at home knew about what had happened was when the police called to the house in the dead of night. The word spreading around the area was that Willie had passed away, but fortunately we had been told differently. Mum and Dad drove down straight away to be with him. When they came back they tried to put a brave face on it. Willie was paralysed from the chest down, but because it appeared he was regaining some feeling in his legs there was a theory that he might recover, and that the paralysis could be down to the shock of the accident. Deep down, I think we all feared the worst. We hoped for the best.

That night, after my parents had come back from their first trip to visit Willie in hospital, the police came knocking at the door again in the early hours. Listening from the top of the stairs, we could hear them telling Mum and Dad that Willie had deteriorated and that he had lost a lot of blood. They had been sent to tell us to prepare for bad news, but he pulled through.

We only had the one car between us, so the brothers and sisters had to take turns to go down and visit. I'll never forget my first trip down the road, going down along with Willie's best friend John McKerracher, to the hospital in Musselburgh where he was being cared for. It was like a scene from a Frankenstein movie, with Willie upside down on a big turntable bed. His head was pinned in and his arms strapped down, as if he was in a straitjacket. Every six hours they would flip the bed over, moving him from facing the floor to facing the ceiling. It was shocking to see and John was physically sick at the sight of it all.

After two or three months in hospital he was well enough to return home. Everyone had to adjust their life after the accident; everything changed. From the physical things like getting the house prepared for a wheelchair, to the emotional side, nothing was ever the same again.

My mother was never the strongest person anyway, but the situation with Willie really took its toll. She had given birth to four big strong boys and all of a sudden one of them had been cut down in his prime. Willie was 6ft 2in tall and a real athlete – he was the fastest of all of us. Neither my big brother David nor myself and the youngest of my brothers, Finlay, could touch him over 100 yards. He had gone from that big strong lad one minute to being unable to do anything for himself the next. It was tragic.

Mum wanted to help so much, but in truth she was helpless. With the best will in the world there was no way she could cope with the heavy lifting of getting Willie in and out of bed, into his wheelchair or getting him bathed. With all her heart she wanted to do those things but she needed help from her boys to do those things. You would find her wandering around Willie's bedroom, downstairs in the big room because it was on the ground floor, plumping his pillows up because it was something she could do for him. It broke her heart and the fact that I was about to follow my brother in flying the nest couldn't have helped, with Dave already playing for Middlesbrough and me on my way to Chelsea.

When the taxi arrived at the house to take me to catch my flight to London, I gave her a big hug and watched as she turned in tears to walk back up the path to the house. What I didn't realise was that she was battling her own issues at the same time as trying her best to come to terms with Willie's situation.

She was a heavy smoker, never without her Capstan Full Strength, and my Dad was the same. That led to problems for Mum and around Christmas time in 1983, just a few months after I'd made the move to London, I got a call at my digs from my aunty to say that Mum had been taken into hospital with collapsed lungs. Obviously I had to get home quickly. I was upstairs packing my bag when the phone rang again. It was another message for me from back home, this time to tell me there was no need to rush back – Mum had passed away already. It was the first time I had been away from home and all of a sudden I felt like I was on the other side of the world.

Nita Hurley, who was my landlady then and later became my mother-in-law, took control of the situation, arranging my flights home and getting me back as soon as possible. It was a shocking time for us all. On top of William's accident, losing Mum was a hammer blow. In my mind I was going back to Fort William for good when I got on that plane. I was sickened by everything and just wanted to get back and do what I could for the rest of the family.

Mum's health had deteriorated but I will always believe that it was a broken heart that claimed her life. To watch one of her big strapping boys confined to his bed, needing help just to wipe his mouth, simply devastated her. She just wasn't strong enough to cope.

When I did get back I ended up drowning my sorrows with my brothers for three or four days – serious drinking with no let-up. I was in a complete daze. Eventually, after a week or so, the Chelsea assistant manager Ian McNeill obviously decided I'd had long enough. He tracked me down and had a good talk with me. He pointed out that there was nothing for me in Fort William, that if I stayed I'd end up going back to the life I had before, with odd jobs here and there and signing on the dole in between. He brought me to my senses and I decided to give it another go with Chelsea. From that point on I never looked back. It had taken two of the most devastating periods in my life to set me on the road but once I took the first few steps I knew I was heading in the right direction.

After the drinking binge in the wake of Mum's death, I didn't touch another drop for a good nine months. Even then, I would only have the occasional pint. I learned that you have to know when to drink and when not to drink – too many people can't make that call for themselves. Even when the boys were going out for a few drinks on a Saturday night after games, I wasn't interested. I decided to knuckle down and give myself the best chance of making a go of it.

It was an absolutely torrid time for the family, which was compounded by the fact that my sister Amanda was involved in a motorbike accident up in Tongue soon after and suffered horrendous injuries. Amanda recovered from that, but the pain of losing Mum was far worse. As the youngest daughter, she'd been particularly close to Mum and it took a long time for the pain to ease.

I was one of seven children but my Dad and brother Finlay – or Midgie, as he's better known – were left at home with Willie. When he first came home from hospital there was a determination to carry on as before, as though nothing had changed. The problem was that it had changed.

If the brothers were going out for a few drinks, Willie wanted to come along. We'd wheel him along in his chair and everyone at the pub was delighted to see him out and about. He was a hell of a pool player as a teenager and a popular guy at our local. We were a big family in Caol, the village where we grew up, well known and well liked. People would go out of their way to speak to Willie and buy him a dram or two, something that didn't mix well with his medication. More than once he suffered relapses and ended up in hospital, needing his stomach pumped to clear the mix of the tablets and alcohol. He still thought he'd be able to have a vodka and Coke or a couple of beers, but soon found out it didn't work that way. Of course we knew it was wrong for him to take a drink, but I don't think we realised the extent of the problems it could cause. Eventually he stopped taking a drink at all and it was for the best. I was so pleased when he made that decision. It is one thing being hungover and ill through drink when you're able-bodied; far worse when you're paralysed and being sick in your bed.

In the early days there were plenty of friends to call round and keep him company, but that tailed off in time and life changed for Willie. Still I never heard him being bitter about it, never heard him blame anybody for the accident.

When it happened, my first reaction was to want to go looking for the taxi driver and give him a beating. It would have done no good at all, but may have made me feel a bit better. I only got as far as mentioning it to my brothers before common sense prevailed, but I'm pretty sure the same thoughts had gone through their heads. That would have only caused more worry for the family because it wouldn't have taken a genius to figure out who was responsible if the guy had landed up in hospital.

To be honest, I couldn't tell you the driver's name. As far as I'm aware I've never met him. I don't even know if it was a genuine taxi. In those days a lot of people went out moonlighting at weekends in their own cars, just slapping a big white sign on the roof. There were no other cars involved and no witnesses, so we'll never know the truth about what happened that night.

From memory the driver was banned from driving for a year and fined for his part in the accident – but I'm guessing he has paid far more than that by living with what he did for all these years. I know it isn't something I would want on my conscience.

All we could do as a family was get on with life and make the best of the hand we'd been dealt. Dad and Finlay looked out for Willie, who had a wee bell to ring when he needed anything. There were home helps to lend a hand and everyone did what they could.

It was difficult to take. He had his whole life ahead of him.

Who knows what he might have gone on to do had he not been cut down in his prime. It was a wake-up call for me and I wanted to make the best of the opportunities that I had.

2

TRIALS AND TRIBULATIONS

I'll never forget sitting on the Scotland team bus after a training session at Greenock and catching the eye of one of the Morton coaches who was loading balls into the boot of his car. It was the old Rangers defender Davie Provan, who was working with the Morton youth team at Cappielow at the time. He looked up and gave me a knowing wink – he remembered me just as much as I remembered him.

The fact that I was sitting there with the national squad was a gentle reminder that he'd got it wrong when he decided I wasn't good enough to make it as a footballer while I was just a teenager. That was when Davie was with Partick Thistle and had the task of taking the young players under his wing at Firhill. To be fair to him, I made it easy for him to cross me off his list of potential professionals.

It was the summer of 1979 when my good friend Alan McKinnon and I were invited down from Fort William to Glasgow for a week's trial with the Jags. Alan had spent the season before with Clach and had shown up well in the Highland League playing as a striker, while I'd been playing away in the Lochaber welfare leagues, still just a lad of sixteen. Partick obviously saw it as a bit of an untapped market and, as well as looking at the pair of us, there was also word of them looking at my brother Willie, who was a fast and strong defender before the road accident shattered any hopes he had of making it in football.

Thistle were going well at the time, established in the Premier Division and building for the future. They had just survived in the top flight, at the expense of Hearts and Motherwell, and had reached the semi-finals of the Scottish Cup when they showed an interest in Alan and me. Looking back, it was a big deal for two young lads to get a chance with a team at that level. To us it was just a bit of an adventure.

What nobody had told Alan and me was that we had arrived just in time for the start of pre-season training. It was a brutal experience for two teenagers still wet behind the ears, but we came through it in one piece as Bertie Auld and his coaching team put the squad through its paces.

Davie Provan, as the coach in charge of us, chose a bed and breakfast on Great Western Road in Glasgow for our digs and we knuckled down and got on with the work. At the end of the week we thought we'd celebrate by having a few beers in our room. We got six cans and it was my first real experience of alcohol – after a couple I was starting to feel the effect, but we didn't cause any bother. When we finished we put the cans in the bin and never thought any more about it. In glorious hind-sight I'd imagine the landlady would have been straight on the phone to Davie the next day to tell him what we'd been up to, although nothing was said.

We were taken up the road to Fort William for a couple of games as part of Partick's Highland tour. I played and scored on the Saturday; Alan played on the Sunday and did well. Despite that, both of us were told 'thanks, but no thanks' at the end of it. They promised to keep an eye on the pair of us, but we all know what that means. To this day I'm convinced our little refreshers in the guesthouse put paid to any chance we had of winning a contract. We were young and didn't know any better.

10

If I had my time again I'd maybe do things differently, but then again everything worked out in the end.

I made a few decisions during those early years, and when I look back I wonder how things might have panned out if I'd done things differently. Turning my back on Sir Alex Ferguson, or plain old Alex as he was back then, is one of them.

That episode began in September 1981, when I was invited down to Aberdeen on trial, after a good run playing for Inverness Clachnacuddin in the Highland League. I should have known it wasn't going to run smoothly when I was involved in a car crash that almost stopped me from getting there in the first place.

John Flannigan, Doug Masson, John Dennison and myself drove through from Lochaber together for Clach games and the day before I was due to join up with the Dons we were motoring through for a match at Buckie when the car hit a stray sheep near Spean Bridge and we ended up ploughing into a ditch. All I saw was a flash of white wool flying past the window before we careered off the road. We scrambled out of the car, which was smashed up pretty badly, but were shaken rather than injured. About forty yards up the road, the poor old sheep hadn't been so lucky – but that didn't stop John Flannigan, our driver, giving it a piece of his mind. He was standing over the carcass, calling it all the names under the sun.

Eventually we got a lift through to the game and made it to Victoria Park with twenty minutes to spare. I dashed through to Pittodrie afterwards, still in a bit of a daze. My Clach team-mate Alex Chisholm went on trial at the same time, with Celtic's scout John Kelman also tagging along to take a look at us around the same time.

I didn't even have a decent pair of boots to take with me for the trial, so Clach dipped into their coffers to put that right. It was just as Alex Ferguson was really starting to make an impact at the club. He had some big characters in his dressing room,

11

and for a young lad from the north it was an intimidating environment to be parachuted into.

The thing that sticks in my mind is how nice John McMaster was to me – he went out of his way to come and talk to me and give me encouragement. He didn't have to do it, but it was a great help in settling me in. It's easy for senior pros to live in a bubble and let the world revolve around them, but John was a class apart. It was a baptism of fire working with Alex Ferguson and Archie Knox. There was no question the pair of them were in charge and even in the week I had with them I knew exactly how big an influence they were on everything at Pittodrie.

I trained away for the week and really enjoyed my time, scoring five in one of the bounce games we played and giving a good account of myself. I went back to Clach on the Saturday but soon enough Alex Ferguson called up the chairman Alistair Chisholm to arrange for me to go down for a second week.

Clach must have been keen to push the deal through because they sent a car to take me to the station to catch the train down. I got word that the reserve game I was due to play in had been postponed and decided to ditch the train to Aberdeen and head for home instead. Maybe I should have gone through anyway but I ducked out of it.

Understandably Mr Ferguson wasn't too pleased – and I don't think my chairman was either. He did his best to smooth things over with Aberdeen but when I turned away from the platform that day the deal was as good as dead.

Being headstrong, I had decided I wasn't going. I had no clean clothes with me and needed to go home and get myself together before I went back. I didn't think too much about it at the time, but in retrospect I can see why the club decided not to give me another chance – they obviously thought I was too big for my boots and weren't going to let me dictate to them. That wasn't my intention, but I can see why they saw it that way.

There was a lot of speculation doing the rounds about exactly what had happened. I guess a lot of people thought I'd fallen foul of Fergie and that I'd stepped out of line, but it was nothing of the sort. Just a case of crossed wires and a misunderstanding that cost me what could have been a golden opportunity.

When I went back in 1992 as a £500,000 player I made a beeline for Teddy Scott's room. He'd looked after me when I was down on trial but I knew I could pull his leg, telling him: 'See Teddy, if you hadn't decided I wasn't good enough all those years ago you could have saved the club a fortune.' He knew I was winding him up, but Teddy insisted it was Drew Jarvie, not him, who'd convinced Sir Alex that I wasn't up to scratch. I'd actually stayed with Drew when I was down, he had a guest house on Great Western Road in Aberdeen, and I'm pretty sure he would have given me a decent reference. Somehow I think Fergie made his own decisions and he clearly didn't think I was keen enough, given I'd hardly walked over hot coals when I'd been asked back for a second week.

It wasn't arrogance on my part, it was just that I had never really seen football as anything more than a hobby. Shinty was really my big passion right through my school days. It wasn't until I turned eighteen or nineteen that I really started to take football seriously, and even then I never really considered it would become my livelihood. I'd played with my school teams and then in the welfare leagues but it was never more than fun for me.

A clutch of guys from in and around Caol had gone on to play professionally. Donald Park, a distant cousin of mine, had made a name for himself with Hibs, George Campbell had gone to Aberdeen and Donny Gillies had played for both of the Bristol clubs, but it wasn't as though there was a senior club on our doorstep. For the size of the village, as it was then, there was a pretty good success rate of providing players for the professional game.

I've often had the debate with Charlie Christie at Caley Thistle about the reasons behind the success of Fort William in producing players compared to Inverness, with its far bigger population and catchment area. That has turned on its head since Ross County and Caley Thistle have been in the senior game, but before then the players coming out of Inverness and going on to play at the top level were few and far between. There were exceptions, with Eric Black and Bryan Gunn feeding through to Aberdeen and the likes of Billy Urquhart and Kevin McDonald being picked up, but for whatever reason there was a better rate of success over in Fort William. When myself and John McGinlay broke through to the international team in the 1990s it put the icing on the cake.

Playing for Scotland had never crossed my mind when I was a wee boy. Kicking a ball around in the park was enough for me. We weren't far from the shops and if I went for a loaf of bread I'd go running through the fields with a ball at my feet.

I went to Caol primary school and I'll always remember the headmaster, Mr Macleod, telling my mum when I was no more than ten years old: 'I'm sorry Mrs Shearer, but I'm afraid your son's brains are in his feet.' Maybe he was right, but it turned out that all I had to do for the bulk of my working life was sign my name on a contract or two. I let my feet do the hard work from the day I got my break with Clach in the Highland League in the late 1970s.

•

3

THE JOURNEY BEGINS

I'm proud to have been part of the story of one of the biggest, or at least the longest, names in Scottish football: Inverness Clachnacuddin. It is perhaps not the most glamorous of clubs, but it was Clach who sent me on the road that took me to some fantastic places in football and I'll forever be grateful for the education I received as a young player at Grant Street Park.

When the club went into administration in 2009 it was a blow for everyone who has a soft spot for the old Lilywhites. It was not the first time the club had been in financial difficulty, but the real fear was that it might be the last. Clach had been saved before but no club has a divine right to survive and the worry was that the latest setback would be one blow too many.

Fortunately, as had been the case in the past, there was a last-gasp effort to keep the team alive and they were able to move out of administration and back onto a more stable footing in time for the 2010/11 season. It meant that Inverness retained a place in Highland League football and that the grand old name of Clachnacuddin was not lost forever. That was the very real fear this time round and it came very close to the wire before a deal was eventually struck to stave off the creditors and clear the debts.

It would have been an absolute travesty if Clach were to have disappeared completely, for the city and for me personally. It's a difficult thing to explain, but when you go back to an old ground where you played before you get flashbacks to big games and important goals. Just standing on the touchline can take you right back to the moment and Grant Street Park holds a lot of good memories for me. I hope in twenty years I'm still able to go back there and relive them, but that will depend on a rapid improvement in fortunes.

There's a tendency to think that a club cannot just disappear – but it has happened to others and there's nothing to say it could not happen to Clach in the future, unless the latest round of administration serves as a serious wake-up call. It doesn't matter how much goodwill there is, it is cold hard cash that keeps a team going. Teams are having to become more and more creative and I don't envy them one bit – there's an awful lot of clubs and organisations, not just in football, competing for a pot of money from sponsors that is hardly overflowing at the moment.

The competition for supporters is far more intense now too. People have plenty of choices when it comes to whiling away a few hours on a Saturday afternoon and football, sadly, isn't at the top of everyone's list.

With Caley Thistle offering senior football just down the road, Clach really are up against it. The enclosure – known as the Wine Shed because the punters would smuggle their bottles in and hide away at the back for a sly drink – used to be packed to the rafters. Now you're lucky if there's half a dozen in there – if it's even open. It has been taped off a lot because of worries about its safety recently. The old grandstand was sold for development after my time there and there have been plans recently to sell off more of the land around the ground for housing. Slowly it's changing and being eroded, but that's football.

The bad times make you appreciate the good all the more and I was fortunate enough to have plenty of those while I was on the books at Clach. Billy Robertson, who had been a goalkeeper and trainer at Grant Street Park, was the manager in those days and Inverness was a good place to play your football.

Caley were the major players at that time, with Clach and Thistle doing their best to challenge. To have three clubs going at it hammer and tongs to get one over on each other made for some interesting derbies. Gates for those games could top 3,000 and it's incredible to think that so many SPL matches can't bring in those numbers today. There were a lot of quality players on the go – people like Dougie Masson and John Flannigan as well as Mitch Bavidge and Bobby Wilson. I still see a fair bit of Bobby around and about Inverness and there's always good craic – it's hard to believe it's thirty years since I started out in the Highland League.

We had a decent set-up at Grant Street Park and a team to match. I had my first experience of a cup final with Clach in the 1979/80 season but it wasn't a happy one. We reached the last two of the North of Scotland Cup against Elgin but I was four-teenth man and never got the call to play. We won the cup, but when you're not part of the team it's not quite the same.

Fortunately when we made it to the Highland League Cup final against Brora two seasons later I had pushed my way into the side. The club had won the league in 1975 but had some lean years after that and it was a big thing to be gunning for the cup.

When the final came around I scored early with a peach of a thirty-yard curling shot. They equalised within a minute but I had the last laugh with a header at the back post to win the cup. It was a great day for Clach and a great night back at the social club too. The pictures of the team celebrating are still on the wall at the ground and I can still picture the goals as though they were yesterday. It turned out to be the last piece of silverware for a decade for Clachnacuddin, so we were right to make the most of it.

They were good days to be a Lilywhites player and it has saddened me to watch the club struggle for survival. They came through the first time, in the 1990s, but when they went into administration again in 2009 it didn't look good at all. I hope they can pull through again, but it's a very different landscape in football now and the support just isn't there to keep clubs alive on admission money alone.

The prospect of the Highland League without a single Inverness team doesn't sit right and I'm delighted Clach were ready to take their place at the table for the 2010/11 season. The city's always had a big part to play in northern football and it would be nice to think that somehow Clach can stand the test of time. Seeing any club founder isn't nice, but when it's one you have such a strong affinity with it's even harder. It isn't just about nostalgia though – Clach have a couple of hundred young-sters under their wing and whatever happens to the club there has to be provision to make sure the next generation are not held back.

For me it was a great place to learn the game. I was playing for my local welfare team in Lochaber, still only sixteen or seven-teen, when John Dennison, who had taken my brother David to Clach previously, fixed me up with a trial match through in Inverness. I was taken across to play against a Fire Brigade select team and scored a couple of goals, doing enough to be invited back. I'd travel to Inverness to play for the Clach reserves in midweek and it snowballed from there for me.

I owe so much to John for putting me on the right track and showing a bit of faith in my ability. He obviously knew what Dave had been capable of and noticed what I was doing in the welfare league in Fort William, which was going great guns at that time. With the pulp mill flourishing, there were about ten strong teams on the go and my side, the Caol Youth Centre, was one of the best. Linhe United were our main rivals and the stan-dard for that level was superb. Fort William didn't have a Highland League side, with the application for membership knocked back time and time again, so the best players in the area really only had welfare football. The Fort William side that eventually made it into the Highland League in 1985 played away in the North Reserve League before then, but to step up a level it was the Inverness teams we had to look towards. Caley and Thistle were both strong sides and pinched a few players from the west but there was a good crop who ended up at Clach over the years.

My debut was at home to Deveronvale. There was a big deal made in the run-up to the game about Vale signing a couple of youngsters on loan from Aberdeen, Ian Porteous and Steve Cowan, but I did my bit to get a share of the headlines and scored to help us to a 2–2 draw.

I played upfront all the way through my school days but I spent a bit of time playing centre-half during my Clach stint. One of our regular defenders got injured and it was me who was drafted in, spending the best part of a season back there. I enjoyed it and had some good games, the best being a Scottish Cup tie down at Albion Rovers during the 1981/82 season. We ended up losing 2–1, with a John Dennison own goal in the last minute scuppering us, but I held my own. It was the first time I'd been to a Scottish Football League ground. It was hardly impressive – in fact I don't think Cliftonhill has changed in decades – but it was a taster at least.

In between training and playing for Clach I was trying my hand at various jobs. It was very much a case of five months in work then a couple on the dole. It wasn't ideal, but it didn't get me down. I left school before I'd done my O Levels and landed up as a tea boy and doing odd jobs for a construction company. My boss all those years ago is now my brother's boss, so it's a small world.

After that I joined a job creation scheme in Fort William. It was basically a big factory where they took us in to teach us bits and pieces of various trades – everything from bricklaying to fencing. I got all of £17.50 a week for that – after giving £5 to Mum there wasn't too much left to play with. I was eventually getting a couple of quid from Clach for playing part-time, so that helped.

All the time I was looking for something that would give me a bit of stability and a job with some prospects. The British Aluminium plant in Fort William employed hundreds of men at the time and has been a big part of the town for as long as most can remember. I had just turned eighteen and was out of work when there was a strike at the plant among the McGregors work-force, who were involved in the construction of the metal plant. A few didn't go back after the industrial action and my dad told me to go up and ask for a job. He said I should ask for Hans McKinnon and tell him who had sent me. I waited around for what felt like an age at the gate before eventually a white van pulled up at the security hut, and the guard told me it was Hans. I went and asked the question but was told there was nothing going. He was about to get back in the van when I shouted over 'My dad was asking after you.' He turned and said, 'Who's your dad?' When I told him it was Dickie Shearer I was in. 'You can start at 9am.' Even then it was all about who you knew, not what you knew. I spent nine months labouring at the plant, doing my best to get as many shifts on the dumper trucks as I could – because it was easier than hauling concrete about the place.

The aluminium plant wasn't the only big employer. The Wiggins Teape pulp mill at Corpach, on the edge of Fort William, was created in the 1960s and employed 450 people at one point. Now all those jobs are gone and the town's starting a new era. The early 1980s saw the pulp mill shut down and although the paper mill survived for another twenty years or so it is gone now. Fort William has changed a lot over the years, especially with the number of newcomers moving to the area to work in those big plants and then the loss of so many of the big employers. As the jobs go, a bit of the soul goes too.

For me, though, being in and out of work proved to be a blessing in disguise all those years ago. There was a five-a-side pitch built near to us in our village of Caol, surrounded by a four-foot wall with a green mesh fence on top of that. It was no bigger than a tennis court but when I was kicking my heels on the dole it became a home from home – I'd stay and practise my shooting until all hours of the morning. If you imagine trying to get to sleep with me crashing balls off the fence at 1am, you'll realise it wasn't always appreciated by my mates who had work the next morning. I wasn't doing it with any great plan in mind. It wasn't a case of trying to make it as a footballer. It was because I loved kicking a ball about. Without realising it, I was giving myself a fighting chance of making a decent career for myself and making sure I'd never have to sign on again. Even now, the technique I developed back then still serves me well when it comes to getting power into a shot.

My form with Clach brought the interest from Aberdeen and that put me on the radar of every other club in Scotland and further afield. Early in 1982, just a few months after my brief time at Pittodrie, I was asked down on trial by Middlesbrough.

Clach said no because we were up against a bit of a fixture backlog at the time, although I think they were also getting fed up with senior clubs taking liberties and expecting the young players to be available at the drop of a hat. I was getting used to having my hopes dashed for one reason or another, so I got my head down again and kept doing my thing. A year later, in February 1983, the hard work paid off when Chelsea came in for me. I'd seen the last of the dole queue and at last I had a profession with prospects.

4

JOINING THE CHELSEA SET

Wembley. It's a name to conjure up all sort of images and magical moments from football down through the years. For me, the first memory is very different and it is of Wembley Station, not Wembley Stadium. It wasn't my finest moment but it did prove very early on that mixing business with pleasure in this game just doesn't work.

The moment of realisation came while I was still a young pro at Chelsea. I was with my first club trying to make the most of a big break. Because I was a late starter in the senior game I couldn't afford to let the chance pass me by; I knew I probably had one shot at making a career for myself.

Within two years of joining Chelsea in 1983 there was a change in management. John Neal, the man who had signed me from Clach, was gone and in his place came John Hollins. I was playing for the reserves and scoring plenty of goals, so John made an effort to get to know me better and took the time to talk away to me.

Inevitably conversation turned to my big brother David, who by that time was with Gillingham. When the Chelsea first team were playing at Stamford Bridge I'd take my place in the stand to watch them, but if they were away from home I'd take the chance to go to one of the other London clubs. I loved going to Spurs, Watford or QPR, visiting all the grounds in the city. I just loved being around so many clubs and making up for lost time watching different teams play, I was like a kid in a sweetie shop.

The manager knew that was how I spent my weekends and couldn't get over the fact that I never went to see my brother play, especially given Gillingham was just along the road from where I was staying at the time. Eventually I relented and went along with John's encouragement to go and see David play. He didn't realise it, but it wasn't the best piece of advice a manager could give his young player. After the game we went for a couple of beers. Saturday night turned into Sunday morning and the session carried on through the day. By the end of the second night I'd never felt so ill, or so drunk.

In between all of that I'd never even thought to call Nita, who was still my landlady at that point, and tell her I was staying with my brother. By Monday morning she was going out of her mind with worry and thought I'd been missing for two nights. She had called Chelsea's training ground to let them know, and there was a huge hoohah going on back at the club.

Oblivious to the panic I'd created, I made my way back across London. That's where my memories of Wembley begin. I was on the underground on the morning after the weekend before and started feeling sick as we pulled into Wembley tube station. I had my hand over my mouth and just as the doors hissed open I threw up all over the platform. Needless to say, I didn't make training that day. Fortunately I managed to redeem myself in the years ahead by making it to Wembley stadium and playing in some memorable games under the famous old Twin Towers, but football was the furthest thing from my mind that day.

Meanwhile, David was hauled into the office of his manager, who was demanding to know, 'Where the hell's your brother? We've had Chelsea on the phone saying he's gone AWOL.' He took a bit of a pasting over that little saga and I was expecting the same when I eventually made it back to training, ready to dig into my pocket to pay a hefty fine. When John Hollins walked in he just said 'Are you okay?' and that was the end of it. I looked at him and said: 'Now you know why I don't go and visit my brother.'

The manager knew that I rarely took a drink. Even if we were at functions where the beer was flowing I was happy to take a back seat. He'd asked me before why I'd stopped drinking and I'd told him it was because I wanted to make it as a footballer. He must have taken that on board and decided to go easy on me. If I'd done it again I'm sure he'd have hauled me over the coals, but I never did.

I was determined not to make some of the mistakes that David did. I knew fine well that he was part of a big drinking culture at the clubs he was at. Deep down I'm pretty sure if he hadn't been wrapped up in that he wouldn't have drifted down the leagues in the way he did. I was determined I wouldn't go the same way and to do that I had to keep my nose clean and stay out of trouble.

Don't get me wrong, David had a hugely positive influence on me. He led the way for me and showed what was possible. Because of that I didn't think twice when Chelsea asked me to sign. I'd seen what my brother had achieved, going down to Middlesbrough and making a name for himself, and wanted the same for me.

David had gone into the Boro team pretty much straight away when he signed for them from Clach in 1978 and he made a big impact – living the dream when he scored against Liverpool at Anfield to show that he could live in the best of company. I'd read the newspaper cuttings from the matches he played in, pick up the football cards with his picture on and try on his Middlesbrough strip for size when he came back over the summer. It was an exciting time for his brothers back home as much as it was for him.

David, the first of the Shearers to try his hand at playing centre-forward, had caught the eye of a few clubs when he was a young lad playing in Lochaber. Hearts and Morton both watched him closely and he signed an S-form at Cappielow before Clach gave him his chance and he grabbed it with both hands, banging in the goals after joining them in the 1976/77 season. The west coast had been a happy hunting ground for the club, which had signed Donnie Gillies previously and moved him on to Morton.

Within a year of playing in the Highland League and averaging more than a goal every other game, David was approached by Willie Ormond at Hearts. Partick Thistle and Aberdeen had also been sniffing around but when Hearts made their interest known it brought things to a head.

Middlesbrough came from nowhere and jumped to the head of the queue. He pretty much went straight into the Boro team as a nineteen-year-old and when he scored twice against Chelsea at Ayresome Park on his debut in the First Division the headlines started getting bigger. He had some great times at Middlesbrough, with an FA Cup double against Arsenal at Highbury among them.

Boro went down in 1982. Dave moved on to Grimsby Town the following year and then Gillingham a season later. He was a big hit with Gillingham, scoring more than a goal in every two games, and Bournemouth paid £20,000 for him in 1987. He stopped off with Scunthorpe, Darlington and non-league Billingham before heading back home and signing for Fort William in 1990. My wee brother Finlay was playing for Fort too, so it was a family reunion on and off the park.

It was John Neal who had signed David for Middlesbrough in 1978 and it was John Neal who came back to the Highlands in 1983 to recruit Shearer No.2, by which time he was in charge at Chelsea. The fact he already knew David helped me settle in at Chelsea. John would forever be asking, 'How's your David?' in that lovely Tyneside accent of his. He thought Dave was a 'canny lad' and knew I was cut from the same cloth.

David was a bit more streetwise than I was by then, given he had a few years of a head start on me in England. It was a whole new world to me. I'd never flown before I got the plane down to London to join Chelsea and I remember clear as day sitting there absolutely terrified by the noise of the take-off. Fortunately for me, I was sitting next to a priest – so I was in safe hands. We got talking on the way down and he wished me well. I've still got a letter that he sent on to Stamford Bridge after everything had gone through to make the move permanent.

Initially I went down and had a couple of days' training before they decided to go ahead and sign me. They put me up in a hotel near the ground for the first night and then moved me to digs in Amersham for the rest of the week. I'd just had time to drop my bag off at the house when Ian McNeill, the assistant manager, came past to pick me up and take me to a reserve game against Bristol Rovers at Eastville. It finished 0–0 and it was the fastest game I'd ever played in my life.

After an hour or so my legs had gone and I was toiling – even my own team-mates were shouting across to Ian to tell him to get me out of there. He didn't though, he kept me on to the bitter end. These boys had all been playing full-time football from the age of sixteen and there was me strolling in after training a couple of nights a week and playing in the Highland League.

At the end of it he took me to one side and asked me how much I thought Clach would be looking for for me. I knew then that I hadn't blown it, that he wanted to keep me at Chelsea. I also knew that Clach wouldn't be difficult to deal with. For one thing, they appreciated that I was flitting in and out of work and there was no way they would stand in the way of me getting full-time employment in football. They were also well aware that

Chelsea would be fair and I think they quickly agreed on a fee of £5,000 upfront, with the same due again once I'd played ten first-team games. I never hit that trigger, but Clach still got the initial fee and it wasn't an insignificant amount in those days – especially for a club that needed every penny it could get. For my part, I was just glad they had got something to recognise the fact they had spent three years bringing me on as a player and giving me a platform to play on. I'll always be grateful for the part they played in my life, right down to buying me my kit for going on trial.

Ian had to dash off after the game and left Clive Walker, a big favourite with the fans at that time, to give me a lift back to my digs. When we got to Amersham, Clive asked me where he should drop me – and it dawned on me that I didn't have a clue.

There were no mobile phones in those days, so we had to find a phone box so Clive could make a few calls. He tried the club and anyone he could think of, but drew a blank. Eventually some-body got hold of Ian McNeill for us, but even Ian didn't know where he'd picked me up from. He'd had the address in the morning on the way to the game but didn't have the bit of paper it was scribbled on. We managed to track it down and eventu-ally get me home. I made a point of keeping the address in my wallet after that, realising that London's a bit more difficult to find your way around than Lochaber.

There was as big a learning curve on the pitch as there was off it. One of my biggest regrets is that I never really had a proper apprenticeship in football. I was a late starter, even in Highland League terms, and then went straight into senior football with Chelsea. In a perfect world it would have been good to have had a couple of stepping stones in between because it's a big change from playing at places like Brora and Rothes to running out at Stamford Bridge and the like. I was twenty-one when I turned professional and there was a lot of time to make up for.

I'm a great believer that for every player there's a single game that turns the whole world for them, either positive or negative. For me it was a good change and it was a game at Victoria Park in Dingwall in a midweek match under the lights.

Clach won 4–2 against Ross County that night and I scored two great goals. Watching from the stand was the late, great Rodwell Clyne. Rod was a big figure in Highland League circles and was very well connected.

He was doing some scouting for Ian McNeill at Chelsea and must have given me a good report. Ian, who was a former Aberdeen player himself, had a lot of joy scouring Scotland for players who weren't going to cost the earth. It wasn't as structured as the academies the English clubs have in place now but there was a pretty good scouting network looking around in the north. Geography didn't hold us back – if you had a bit of talent you had a fighting chance of being noticed by one of the big teams from south of the border.

When I went to Chelsea they were a club in transition. John Neal had only been in charge for a season and a half by that time and his side was toiling to get out of the old Second Division and back into the big league. The good times were just about to roll though. In my first full season the top team won the Second Division championship and after that were in the top six in the First Division, pushing for Europe.

The drawback for me was that the success of the first team meant the opportunities for me were few and far between, especially since David Speedie and Kerry Dixon very rarely missed a game through injury. I made my debut in February 1986 against Leicester at Stamford Bridge. That day both Kerry and David missed out, so it was myself and Paul Canoville who led the line. I scored one of the goals to settle my nerves and I got a run-out in the next game against Oxford United before the main men returned and I was bumped back down to the reserves.

It was hard to take in one sense – but in another I'd done what I set out to achieve. To come from where I'd come from, make it into the Chelsea team in the old First Division and get my first goal was a massive achievement.

My next game for the first team was on Valentine's Day in 1986 and it came at Ibrox. It felt like I'd leapt straight from Grant Street Park in Inverness to playing at one of the country's best stadiums and it was an exciting time for me. The game had been arranged as the second half of a double-header raising money for the Bradford City disaster fund. Chelsea rested quite a few of the big names for the game up in Glasgow, so myself and some of the other fringe players were drafted in. My brother Finlay drove through from Fort William for the game with Alan McKinnon, Gogo Blackmore and Norman Bruce.

We were beaten 3–2 by Rangers on a wintry night, but getting that first taste of top-team football made up for the result. Because I didn't get many chances to return home, I arranged with John Hollins not to go back with the team. Instead he gave me permission to have a few days off and go back with Finlay and the boys to Fort William.

We left Govan at about 10.30pm and made our way through the snow to Loch Lomond on the way home. We were not far from Arracher when we hit a dip in the road. Finlay was driving and put his foot on the brake. Nothing happened. He pulled on the handbrake. Nothing happened. The road was like a sheet of ice and we soon realised we were in trouble, sliding towards the loch and bracing ourselves for the inevitable. The car hit a little barrier at the foot of the slope, rolled onto its roof and went crashing towards the water. Somehow it stopped on the bank and we all clambered out to safety.

We started wandering along the road until eventually we were spotted and taken back to a nearby hotel to get warmed up.

There was a Valentine's dance on, but we weren't in the mood for a party. It was a hair-raising experience and if we'd ended up in the water on that freezing night there wouldn't have been much chance of getting out of that car.

Finlay had been doing no more than twenty miles per hour and when the police came to take him back to the scene of the accident they knew exactly where to go. It turned out there had been an incident at the same spot earlier in the night, with the car hitting the barrier then and obviously weakening it. When we slid into it there was no way it was going to take the weight of the car.

We had a few drinks to calm our nerves while we waited for our cousin, Andy Gow, to come through from Fort William in his big van to take us home. It was a hell of a memorable end to the day.

It was good to finally be edging up the pecking order, but even before I'd made it into the team I'd started to make an impression. Within three or four months of arriving there was an approach from Reading. John Hollins, who was the first team coach at that point, told me he felt it would be better for me to stay and continue to learn with Chelsea. I took his advice and never regretted it.

All I could do was play away and keep doing my best for the second string. We won the reserve league championship and I chipped in with twenty-eight goals on the way to that title. Further down the line the impact I made at that level proved to be key in earning me regular football elsewhere.

In the meantime, I was learning my trade in great company. The first team and the reserves trained separately, although we sometimes had our numbers bolstered by the under-nineteens working with us. That was an eye-opener in itself – I was five or six years older than a lot of them, but the standard was phenomenal. Gwyn Williams took the under-nineteens and they had just won the FA Youth Cup, with so many talented players in that squad.

Gwyn was a tremendous coach and went on to become a big part of the success the club had, working under the likes of Gianluca Vialli, Ruud Gullit and then Jose Mourinho as chief scout. He's credited with discovering John Terry, amongst others, but the crop of youngsters he had back in the early 1980s must have been as good as any of the groups he helped produce. For me it was a challenge to bring myself quickly up to speed as a full-time pro and I like to think I held my own, bringing my own qualities to the mix.

Chelsea was an interesting club to be around in the early 1980s, on all fronts. I'd gone from Inverness Clachnacuddin to Stamford Bridge, one of the trendiest teams in Britain in the most glamorous part of London. I knew about that part of the club's reputation, but was totally oblivious to some of the other aspects of life with the Blues. I soon found out though.

I lived in digs throughout my time in London, staying with the same family I had lodged with when I first landed in England on trial. Mark, my landlady's son, was around the same age as me and keen on his football. What I didn't realise was that he was good friends with some members of the original Chelsea crew, the hardcore group of casuals who were in the middle of the 1980s hooligan scene.

I never twigged until he invited me along to a Chelsea away game up at Leeds. Without hesitation I agreed to go along and, before I knew it, I was crammed in an Intercity football special heading north – me and hundreds of Chelsea fans head to toe in Pringle and Burberry gear, the uniform of the casuals.

Very few of Mark's mates really knew who I was or what I did – only a few of them found out I was a young Blues player. I was just another face in the crowd for most of them. We got all the way up to Yorkshire before the talk started to turn to meeting up for fights. I remember thinking 'this is a bit strange', then it started getting more and more boisterous.

By the time we had to get off at Doncaster to change trains there was a real edge to the atmosphere. Then we found ourselves on our own, with the train for Leeds heading off and leaving about a dozen of us stranded there on the platform. We turned round to see hundreds of supporters marching through the gates in the distance, heading straight towards us. The whispers started going round the group – we were about to come head-to-head with the Leeds mob.

One of the guys turned to me and said: 'We're Chelsea, we don't run from anyone.'

I just thought 'bugger that, I'm quicker and fitter than the lot of you and I'm running for my life'. It was terrifying, until the big group got closer and the whispers started going round 'they're Chelsea, they're Chelsea'. Sure enough, when the two groups met it turned out to be a crew up from London for the game.

Mind you, to say they were up for the football is maybe over-stating things. When we eventually made it through to Elland Road I don't think any of them saw a ball being kicked. They were far too busy barracking the Leeds fans, trying to kick down the fence keeping the fans apart and generally baying for blood. For the record it finished 1–0 thanks to a Kerry Dixon goal, which didn't do much to relieve the tension around the ground.

There were police horses all over the place when we had arrived in Leeds and we were herded into the ground like animals. All around me there were people desperate to get at each other. I was like a wreck by the time we got back to London – my body felt like it had done a week of pre-season training. I'm just glad I came through it in one piece and without getting arrested.

When I went into training at the start of the week I told some of the boys what had happened and their jaws just about hit the floor. They all wanted to hear the stories, though.

Eventually John Hollins pulled me to one side and gave me some friendly words of warning, explaining how bad the troubles were and suggesting I steer clear of hanging out with the casuals in future.

He told me which games it was wise to go to and which ones it wasn't. Back then just about every club had their own mob – but Chelsea was by far the biggest and one of the most feared of the lot.

Following his advice was easier said than done. On match days, when I wasn't involved in the first-team squad, I was in the routine of heading to a little café on the edge of the Fulham Broadway tube station. I'd have a bit of lunch and then stroll down the road to Stamford Bridge for the game. I'll always remember sitting there one Saturday afternoon when Vincent, the owner, offered me a slice of apple pie and cream. I passed on the pudding and made my way out of the door – before I felt Vincent's hand on my shoulder, hauling me back in the door. Before I knew what was happening he'd locked the door, with everyone still inside the café, and pulled the metal shutters down. I thought it was a hell of a length to go to to sell a bit of apple pie, but it turned out that he'd spotted trouble brewing and by the time the shutter fell into place a pitched battle was going on outside, with police sirens wailing and guys in riot gear desperately trying to restore order. It was just another Saturday afternoon in Chelsea.

While I steered clear of those little trips after the Leeds incident, I wasn't totally divorced from the whole casual scene. I'd often share a car through to games with some of Mark's mates – then sit for an hour reading the papers, parked up outside Victoria Station and the like, while those of them who were mixed up in the casual scene went off to meet up with other mobs to fight. Like so many who were caught up in that way of life, Mark's now a successful businessman and leading a life a million miles from those days. That was the thing with the casuals – on the face of it they were smart young boys, but behind that they were dead set on looking for trouble.

It was around that time that Ken Bates, our chairman, came up with the bright idea of putting up electric fences at Stamford Bridge. Every time the ball hit it you heard it fizz – so I'd hate to think how it felt if you had the misfortune to be pressed up against it. Needless to say, the electric fence didn't last too long before they had to take it down.

The atmosphere was phenomenal for the big games. There was one game in particular, when we beat Leeds 5–0 at Stamford Bridge after winning the league in 1984 and gaining promotion from the Second Division. I remember looking round towards the Leeds fans and seeing them ramming a big metal pole into the electric scoreboard. It was bedlam. The referee actually blew for full-time five minutes early because he was so worried about what was going on around him.

You had the Leeds fans on one side intent on causing mayhem and on the other there were the Chelsea supporters lining up on the touchline ready for war. For the last chunk of the match, all of the play was down one side of the pitch – Joey Jones, a player I became great friends with at Stamford Bridge, had told the Leeds boys that it would be in their best interests to stay away from the Chelsea crew and maybe not surprisingly they took his advice. The ball never strayed onto the wing where the masses were gathering ready to charge.

It was all part and parcel of being a Blues player and I came away with so many memories. I will always have a soft spot for Chelsea because it was them who gave me my big break. They are also a wonderful club for looking out for their former players, even those like me who only played a couple of first-team games.

My time in football was not without pain along the way and in 2008 I found myself in considerable discomfort through wear and tear. The doctors decided I needed my right hip replaced and after talking to the PFA in England I discovered they would pay half of the cost to have the operation done privately, leaving me to pay around £5,000 for the remainder.

What I didn't realise was that the PFA had also contacted Chelsea, who run an excellent former players' club and benevolent fund. Without hesitation they offered to pick up the tab for my share of the bill.

Within days of Chelsea making that gesture, I got an appointment through from the NHS and I only faced a wait of three weeks. With that in mind, I cancelled the plans to have the surgery done privately and waited my turn. I know Chelsea were a bit taken aback when I contacted them to say I wouldn't be accepting their money. I suppose a lot of people would have taken the money without hesitation. They really appreciated my response, so much so that the chairman Bruce Buck invited my son William and me down to Stamford Bridge as their VIP guests, which was a fantastic gesture and brilliant for William – who is a diehard Chelsea fan.

I had my hip replaced in 2008 and will probably need my left one done at some point in the future. It's a big improvement and I'm still able to play five-a-side football and get around the pitch. The doctors had never carried out a hip replacement on someone as young as me and they found an awful lot of wear on the joint, but that's a small price to pay for the satisfaction I got from my career.

Playing for Chelsea was a life-changing period for me in so many ways – not least because I didn't just gain a career through my move to London. I also met the woman I have spent the rest of my life with.

Michele, who became my wife in June 1989, is the daughter of Nita and Michael Hurley. It was the Hurleys who took me in as their lodger when I moved from Fort William to London.

They were a big Chelsea-supporting family and Michael was an executive club member. He had got talking to John Neal, who mentioned they had a young Scot coming down to sign. Without even meeting me, Michael volunteered to put a roof over my head. A few months later, they did the same for Kevin McAllister when he moved from Falkirk to Chelsea. Crunchie and I had some great fun living together back then. He made an impact straight away, like a Pat Nevin Mark 2 in the way he played the game. The Chelsea fans took to Crunchie in a massive way.

Michael and Nita were a huge support to me through some very difficult times, particularly the death of my mother. Having that environment was a big factor in helping me to settle and their son and daughter, Mark and Michele, became great friends of mine.

Michele was already engaged but decided to get a fresh start and move away. She had friends who had moved to Aberdeen and she followed them up the road, landing a job with BP. It turned out to be the first of three moves to the city for her. We went back twice after we were married when I went to Pittodrie as a player and then assistant manager.

It was after she had moved to Aberdeen that we first became an item. We kept in touch and eventually she said in a letter that she viewed me as more than just a friend. It blossomed from there as a long-distance relationship before we finally set up home together after I'd moved to Huddersfield. The heart of Yorkshire was very different from the centre of Knightsbridge, but Huddersfield was a whole new chapter in my life and proved to be the making of me as a man and a player.

5

FROM CITY TO TOWN

For some players the prospect of leaving a club the size of Chelsea would be one that would cause sleepless nights. When it was my time to leave Stamford Bridge I didn't have time to worry, it all happened so quickly. I made the decision in seconds and it turned out to be one of the best choices of my career.

It was transfer deadline day in March 1986 when it all happened. Joey Jones, my old Chelsea team-mate, was playing up at Huddersfield Town by then and he persuaded his manager, Mick Buxton, to take a chance on me.

It wasn't a total shot in the dark, mind you. I'd scored goal after goal for the Chelsea reserves, including a hat-trick up at Swindon when we won the reserve championship. I found out later that Lou Macari had tried to take me to Swindon after that game but he missed out and it was Huddersfield who sealed the deal.

Mick paid £10,000 for me and increased my wages from the £140 a week Chelsea were paying me to £240. It wasn't a king's ransom but it was a big improvement and a good move from that point of view. I never even dreamt of using an agent then, feeling I could do the job myself. When you aren't earning fortunes, giving ten per cent to a middle man isn't appealing.

I couldn't even have pointed to Huddersfield on the map before I moved there, but I took the time to speak to Joey about the club and the town and he had plenty of good things to say. I also sounded him out about the wage structure and he pointed me in the right direction when it came to settling the contract. At that stage in my career it wasn't about money for me – it was a chance to get regular first-team football and test my mettle in competitive games.

I was sad to leave Nita and Michael behind, but not so sorry to say goodbye to London, mainly because I absolutely loved life in Yorkshire once I got there. My time in Huddersfield was fantastic. The people were a joy and I couldn't fault the place.

The club was still at its old Leeds Road ground in those days and it was night and day from what I was used to at Chelsea, where everything was done for you and the players were pampered with immaculate kit and everything on a plate. At Huddersfield it was a bit earthier, but at the same time it made for a great spirit around the place. The Leeds Road stadium was sold in 1994 and is a retail park now, but I've still got my memories of the old place. It had a couple of huge stands and the Town fans could generate a real noise for the big games.

I went into digs before eventually buying my own wee house and I settled in an instant, going straight into the team. There were a few games left in the season and the club was fighting against relegation. My first match was Barnsley away, a local derby and one that was big for the manager Mick Buxton as it was against his home-town team. Mick was a proud Yorkshireman, a real salt-of-the-earth type but also a very intelligent football man. I was desperate to do well for him.

I scored a hat-trick, we won 3–1 and I was off and running. The next game was at home to Stoke City and I scored two in a 2–0 win. Everything I touched hit the back of the net and just having somebody to put the ball away gave the whole team a lift. We pulled clear of the relegation zone, I kept scoring goals and it was a good end to the season.

Unfortunately the next season brought more relegation worries and it cost Mick Buxton his job halfway through the campaign. I loved playing for Mick and it was tough to see him pack his bags. He'd been with the club for more than eight years and it was sad it had to end on a low note, with the team still battling away at the wrong end of the table.

Steve Smith, who had been in charge of youth development, took over the first team for a few months but it was never going to last. Steve was a nice guy, but not cut out for management at that level. It's one thing being a good coach and working with the kids, but another to go into a senior dressing room and contend with the egos and characters you find at every club. You've also got the eyes of the support burning into the back of you at every turn and it's not for everyone.

There was one game in particular where we were looking around the dugout for Steve but he was nowhere to be seen. I went up the tunnel and found him with his back to the wall, bumping his head back and forth off the concrete. He told me he wasn't enjoying it at all and it wasn't a major surprise when he was replaced just a couple of months into the 1986/87 season.

He was only in the job for nine months, but he did have a big hand in the direction my career took. At the end of my first full season with Huddersfield, in the summer of 1987, Leeds United came in with a £300,000 bid for me.

Leeds had been my favourite team as a kid and they were still an attractive proposition when the offer came in. Steve was honest about the situation – they didn't want to sell me, not least to their Yorkshire rivals. I was disappointed, but I wasn't going to stamp my feet and sulk about it. On the back of that interest, I renegotiated my contract to get a bit more money and then carried on as I had before. As long as you're doing your job well the rewards tend to come and I was beginning to climb up the ladder.

Steve Smith wasn't around to benefit from the decision to keep hold of me and Malcolm McDonald was the man the board chose to take over, presumably looking for a big name to try and pull a few more supporters through the gates.

At first things were great, but they quickly went downhill. The first nail in the coffin as far as my own relationship with Malcolm was concerned came in the aftermath of the worst game I've ever been involved in.

We went to Maine Road to play Manchester City in the league in the winter of 1987. For a start we looked like bruised bananas, playing in the most horrible black and yellow kit you'll ever see. We didn't play any better than we looked and were 9–0 down as the clock ticked down. Andy May scored a penalty for us to make it 9–1 and then City went up the park with a few one-twos and knocked in their tenth. It was an embarrassing night all round, with Paul Stewart, Tony Adcock and David White all scoring hat-tricks. I've no idea who went away with the match ball that night but I do know we barely got a touch of it.

The next day we were hauled into a function suite at the ground to go over the video nasty of the night before. Practically the first thing we saw was a ball played up to me, early in the match, which got away from me. Without saying a word, Malcolm rewound the tape. Then he did it again, and again, and again. He must have gone back over that one passage of play six times without uttering a sentence of explanation. Then eventually he muttered: 'It's fucking pish.' I said nothing, knowing fine well he had a thing about strikers. Nobody was ever going to be good enough for him playing in that position and he obviously felt he could do a better job himself.

The galling thing was him picking over one lost ball that really didn't cost us anything, right at the start of the game. It wasn't as if City went up the park and scored from it. Given we went on to concede ten goals, I felt there may have been more pressing concerns to address in other departments of the team that night. Maybe he should have been having a look at the defence, the goalkeeper and the midfield for a start. But he was the boss.

It was sod's law that when the FA Cup draw was made we came out of the hat with Manchester City. It was one of those moments when your first reaction is, 'Oh my God, not again' – but then as you start to think more about it you realise that it's a great chance to put right the wrongs of the previous game. We played them at home and with two minutes to go were leading 2–1. I scored both of our goals to put us in front and we were powering on towards what would have been a really satisfying win until they equalised through John Gidman.

We went back through to Maine Road and eventually went down 2–1 in the replay back at our place, but at least a bit of pride was restored and the ghosts of that night were laid to rest. It doesn't matter how many good games you play or how many you win, the ones that tend to linger in your memory are the painful ones. I can still remember that 10–1 defeat like it was yesterday.

We bounced back from that experience to an extent, but there was nothing that could be done to salvage the mood between the manager and me. The most ridiculous episode came after I missed a week of training through illness. By the end of it I was feeling well enough to get out of the house and take in a game. My own side were away from home, so I decided to take the chance to go and watch my brother playing for Scunthorpe over at Halifax.

It was just up the road and I couldn't see the harm in it – unlike good old Malcolm McDonald. He saw a picture of me in the crowd in the evening paper and went absolutely ballistic. He was accusing me of all sorts, saying if I was well enough to go to the game I must have been well enough to train. It was nonsense, but he wouldn't see reason. He fined me the maximum, two weeks' wages, for going to watch my brother play football.

I told him there and then that it was obvious he didn't like me and that I liked him even less, so we may as well leave it at that and not try to get on. I'd been around heavy drinkers all my life and I knew when I was dealing with one. I believe he confronted that problem later in his life, but I can only go on what I saw of him. You could even smell the drink on Malcolm at training and I just couldn't respect him, not just because of that but because of his attitude towards me. It's the one and only time I've felt like that in football and the only time I've been glad to see a manager lose his job.

He was a man I disliked intensely. I've been in plenty of dressing rooms over the years when I haven't agreed with what's being said – when I've nodded my head and let it go in one ear and out the other. With Malcolm I couldn't hide the way I felt and we were never going to get on.

With that one exception, I've always given every coach I've worked with the benefit of the doubt and the respect they deserve. There have been times when I've worked with people who have done far less in the game than me, but that doesn't mean I haven't been able to learn from them.

It infuriates me when players can't see past a manager's playing history. I've seen plenty who just wouldn't listen to anyone they didn't feel deserved their attention. I found this was particularly true back in the Highland League in later years, when I was in charge of Buckie. I could speak from a good position because I'd played for Scotland and scored plenty of goals, but it would irritate me beyond belief when players treated others with less respect.

Malcolm's contribution was to get Huddersfield relegated from the Second Division to the Third Division in the 1987/88 season, which turned out to be my last at the club. We toiled away all year, only winning half a dozen games and stayed rooted to the bottom of the table for all but a few weeks.

All I could do was keep plugging away and try to turn things around. We scored forty-eight goals that season and I got sixteen of them, so I did my bit. It just wasn't enough. My last game was at Leeds Road against Oldham. It was a 2–2 draw and I scored our first. I didn't know at that point that I wouldn't play for Huddersfield again but that was the way it turned out.

Malcolm's assistant, Eoin Hand, took over and went on to have a bit more success in the years ahead. I had moved on by then but it was no more than the fans deserved. They were fantastic to me when I was at Leeds Road and I'll never forget the way they took me to their hearts.

6

SUSPICIOUS MINDS

Football has had its share of murky rumours and sensational headlines over the years. The difficulty is that it's so difficult to separate fact from fiction – or even to decide whether there's any foundation to your own suspicions when it comes to some of the underhand dealings that must have always gone on and probably still do.

I've had brushes with one of the game's big issues: match fixing. Or at least I might have done. To this day I have no idea whether it was a case of my imagination working overtime or whether there were darker forces at play.

I can remember vividly playing one vital game for Huddersfield in one of our annual relegation battles. It was a game we had to win to have any hope of staying up. We were playing a side already promoted and in the warm-up one of their biggest names came jogging over. He pointed out that if we stayed up then it would land one of their big rivals in the mire and signed off by saying, 'Don't worry lads, you'll have no trouble from us.' We won comfortably that day and it didn't look as though the opposition tried a leg. They had already won promotion by that point and were flying out the next day for a big party overseas – they had also stayed up the night before and I reckon had started the celebrations early. I will never know whether we won by accident, because they had their party hats on by then, or by design.

But I will always have my suspicions that something wasn't quite right that day. Never before or after did I experience anything even close to that.

The mechanics of my move from Huddersfield to Swindon Town in 1988 also set alarm bells ringing for me. My manager at Leeds Road, Eoin Hand, pulled me into his office and told me that West Brom were interested at the end of the miserable 1987/88 season, when we had been relegated to the Third Division. There had been an offer that was acceptable to Eoin and the club, so I was free to speak to them and I was left in no doubt that this was a move that I was being encouraged to make.

I arranged to meet Ron Atkinson, who was then in charge at West Brom, and drove through to his house in Birmingham. Big Ron was everything I imagined he would be, from the minute he shook my hand and I saw the row of gold rings on his fingers. He showed me round his house, with a five-a-side pitch in the back garden for the summer barbecues he hosted. I met his wife and was made to feel really welcome – Ron was a larger-than-life character and a really persuasive man.

He told me that Cyrille Regis had been West Brom's last real No. 9 and that he saw me as the next one. I was really being sold the club in terms of the potential there was at the Hawthorns. This was a side that was trying to build a team to get back up to the top division and the manager knew all about the potential for big crowds and success from his previous time in charge.

I got the impression I'd be a big part of what he was planning and he offered me a really good deal – terms that blew away what I was on at Huddersfield. I came away from that meeting feeling pretty keen to sign for West Brom – then the phone rang and everything changed.

On the line was Chic Bates, who was Lou Macari's assistant at Swindon Town. Obviously Lou had been interested when I left Chelsea a couple of years previously and it turned out he had been tracking me ever since. Chic told me that they wanted to take me to Swindon but they had been refused permission to speak to me by Huddersfield. He said: 'They say we can't talk to you unless we match West Brom's offer – but they won't tell us what it is. Duncan, you need to find out that price for us.'

I went back to Eoin Hand and again he appeared desperate for me to sign for West Brom. It was overwhelming, to the extent that he refused point-blank to tell me what they had offered for me. He kept saying over and over again, 'What do you need to know that for?' and 'What the hell does it matter to you?'. He wouldn't give it up.

I said: 'Eoin, it's pretty simple. If you don't tell me the price then how can I negotiate a decent contract? If they're offering £100,000 then that's one thing. If they're offering £500,000, then I'd say I've got a good case for getting a really decent deal.'

Eoin effed and blinded, telling me to get out of his office. I went away and reported back to Chic to tell him the bad news – there was no way I was going to squeeze the price out of Eoin. The more I spoke to the manager the more convinced I became that, for reasons only he knows, there was a determination that I would go to West Brom ahead of any other club.

Maybe he thought West Brom was a wonderful club; it could be that he and Ron Atkinson were best mates. Who knows what was happening behind the scenes? But there's no doubt that Eoin's attitude in trying to push me towards West Brom made me determined not to go to the Hawthorns.

In the end, Swindon decided they would ditch the rule book. They asked me down to speak to them even though they didn't have permission from Huddersfield. I drove down to Wiltshire and met up with Lou, Chic and the chairman Brian Hillier. They told me their plans for me and did a good job of convincing me that the County Ground was the right place for me to play my football.

I also got some pretty valuable financial advice into the bargain. Lou said to me: 'You haven't earned a lot of money from football yet have you? When you go back to Huddersfield, tell them you aren't moving anywhere unless you get a slice of the transfer fee. You cost them buttons, have given them good service and scored a lot of goals – it's only fair they look after you. Think of a figure and ask for it – any amount you like.'

I'd never heard anything like it, but the more I thought about it the more it made sense. Huddersfield were about to make a major profit on me and why shouldn't I get a share of it? So I went back, chapped on Eoin's door and as we spoke it eventually came out that West Brom were ready to pay £230,000 for me. I never even got round to speaking about my share. I turned on my heels and went away to call Lou.

He said that sort of figure was no problem to Swindon and that they'd go straight in and top it. I went back to Eoin and laid my cards on the table: I'd spoken to Lou and Swindon, I wanted to join them and I wanted a cut of the transfer fee. I was half expecting to get a kettle in my face, but I think he knew I was in the driving seat. All I had to do was dig my heels in, refuse to go anywhere and the club would be stuck without getting anything for me. I told Eoin I wanted £20,000 and got up and left – not before Eoin had let me know in no uncertain terms what an unbelievable decision it was not to sign for West Brom.

Pretty soon after I got a call from Keith Longbottom, the Huddersfield chairman. He said: 'Duncan, what have you done to Eoin? He's in a terrible rage.' Again, I went through it with Keith. I said: 'I've scored a lot of goals, goals that have helped keep the club in the division. I've never been more than one of the middle earners and I think it's fair that I get some sort of bonus for the work I've done.'

In the end he had to agree. We settled on £15,000 and I had Lou Macari to thank for making my bank balance look a whole lot healthier. Lou told me to go and get a letter signed by the club secretary confirming the slice of the transfer fee I was due – and the secretary wasn't happy about that. He claimed he knew nothing about it and that there was no way anyone would agree to something like that. After a phone call to the chairman, he reluctantly agreed to type it out and sure enough in my next pay packet there was £15,000 extra.

For the sake of the fans I didn't want it to get messy, but I was fighting for what I was entitled to and I've no regrets about the way I handled it. Football's a short career and you have to look out for your own interests, just as the club will always look after itself.

It all worked out as I hoped it would. Swindon paid £250,000 to get the striker they wanted, Huddersfield got the money they needed to keep the bank manager happy and I was joining a club with big ambitions.

Lou Macari had been in charge for four seasons by then, taking over in 1984 when they were rooted in the bottom league. He won the Fourth Division championship in his second season, promotion from the Third Division in the 1986/1987 season and established Swindon in the Second Division after that.

It was a club geared for success and with a real chance of challenging for the title. There was a good squad in place and a manager who was determined to keep progressing. Having been constantly fighting at the wrong end of the table with Huddersfield, it was going to be a whole new ball game.

Fast forward a year or so, to the end of my first season with Swindon. I was on a plane coming back from my summer holidays when one of the other passengers broke the news to me: 'I see your team's looking for a new manager. Lou Macari's gone to West Ham.' It was the first I knew about it and was totally out of the blue. My reaction? All I could think was 'You beauty!'

It wasn't that I didn't like Lou, I did, he was a great guy. The problem was I just couldn't play for him. Everything from his training to the style of play he adopted just didn't work for me. If Lou hadn't left Swindon Town when he did, then I most certainly would have done. And if I had, I would have missed what I would class as the best days of my career. The year that followed turned out to be a dream for me on the park.

It wasn't like that for me when Lou was in charge. Not to put too fine a point on it, I had a nightmare that year.

It's a shame it worked out that way because Lou was one of the main reasons I signed for Swindon in the first place. Whether it was because he was Scottish or because I knew all about him as a player I don't know, but I found him easy to get on with and very persuasive. The decision to reject West Brom and sign for Swindon was mainly down to Lou and certainly wasn't financial. I never even talked terms fully with Ron Atkinson because I had my heart set on Swindon.

The next time I saw big Ron was when we lost 2–0 at the Hawthorns and I was hooked after an hour. He didn't gloat – far from it. He caught up with me in the tunnel and said: 'Are you okay, kid?' It was a nice touch, but I have to admit I was questioning my decision at that point.

What I didn't realise before signing for Swindon, or until my first training session, was how big Lou was on fitness work. The ball became a bit of a stranger when Lou was in charge because he wanted every member of the squad at the peak of their physical power. There's nothing wrong with that and you can't argue with the results he had, taking Swindon from the Fourth Division right up to the Second Division. His approach was right for the players he had in his squad – just not necessarily for me.

I'd looked at Lou, a man I respected and liked, then looked at Swindon sitting up at the top end of the table and decided it was the right club for me. What I hadn't given any thought to was their reputation as a long-ball team. As I soon found out, it was all about turning the ball over and getting it from back to front as quickly as possible. If there was an offside decision against the opposition on the edge of our box, the ball was placed and the free kick lumped forward before the other side had time to lift their heads.

I really struggled to fit into that system. I had developed a happy habit of scoring on my debut – I did it for Clach, Chelsea, Huddersfield, Blackburn, Aberdeen and Caley Thistle. Swindon was the odd team out and I went for ten games before I eventually scored.

Going into the 1988/89 season, I was their record signing and not surprisingly the supporters were wondering what they had invested in. I was also another member of the growing Scottish colony, joining Colin Calderwood and Ross MacLaren, who had just joined from Derby County. The worry was that they felt it was a case of jobs for the boys under Lou.

Pre-season had actually gone as well as it could have. I scored ten goals in seven games and was confident of hitting the ground running, not least because the first competitive game was at Oakwell against Barnsley. I'd scored twice there on my Huddersfield debut and I went on to score there again when I made my debut for Blackburn Rovers.

It wasn't to be with Swindon, though. I kept thinking the first goal would come, but it didn't. For five long weeks I waited, and for five long weeks it just wouldn't fall for me. In between, I was running myself into the ground, tackling the six-mile road runs that were part of the training programme. We'd go on those runs on a Thursday and the next day my calves would be killing me, with my legs still heavy by the time Saturday's game rolled round.

By the time Lou was appointed as Celtic manager I was at Aberdeen. Quite a few of the Celtic boys approached me to ask what to expect – all I could tell them was to look out their running shoes. There was never any doubt that it would be hard work for them and it wasn't a great surprise that it didn't work for Lou at Parkhead. He didn't really embrace the old free-flowing Celtic style.

Lou would take us off to army camps for training. We'd eat in the mess and the portions were just tiny. You'd get nothing to eat and then be expected to slog your guts out in training. I remember Colin Calderwood picking up a fruit salad and Lou snatching it back from him, saying 'You don't need that, Colin.'

My other abiding memory is settling into my dormitory and finding Dave Hockaday unpacking sandwiches, chocolate and all manner of goodies from his bag. I asked him what on earth he was up to and he said: 'You'll see.' Soon enough, I did.

We had the farcical situation of guys escaping to go and stock up on food from the shops and smuggle it back in. One of the soldiers in the mess would even slip us a box of Mars bars to keep us going.

It was difficult to get out for those illicit food runs. Lou was naturally suspicious about anyone trying to leave the camp. We found that the best way to get out was to tell him you wanted to go out and put a few lines on the horses at the bookie's. That way he let you away in a shot.

I look back at photographs from that time I spent under Lou at Swindon and can't believe how thin I looked. My game has always been about power more than pace and a quick glance at those pictures tells its own story about how the training regime impacted on me.

Mind you, it's amazing my confidence didn't fall as low as my weight during that first season at the County Ground. I remember playing one game against Chelsea when the Swindon fans started to boo me after just twenty minutes. They wanted me hooked there and then. Lou kept faith in me, though, and I scored the equaliser in a 1–1 draw.

That wasn't my first goal, though. I'd got off the mark in a game at home to Crystal Palace when the ball came through to me. I flicked it up and volleyed it – straight at the keeper. Somehow he let it squirrel away from him and it rolled in. It wasn't a classic, but it opened the account. That was a League Cup tie at the end of September and it felt like a lifetime since I'd joined Swindon. That goal was a long time coming but I scored again a few days later in a league win at Watford and then got that equaliser against Chelsea the following week to set things in motion for me.

It was a tough old season, but Lou stuck with me. I ended up as the leading scorer with sixteen goals, three ahead of Steve White, but it hadn't clicked for me properly. The team was something similar – we'd plugged away in mid-table for the bulk of the campaign but finished with a flourish, unbeaten in the last eight to climb into the play-off places.

Chelsea, with ninety-nine points, ran away with the league, but beneath them there was a fierce pack fighting it out for the other promotion spots. Manchester City came through to take the second automatic spot, on eighty-two points, and the play-off places went to Crystal Palace, who were just a point behind City, and then Watford, Blackburn and Swindon. On seventy-six points we scraped into the play-offs in sixth place and that set us up for a semi-final against Palace.

We won the first leg at our place 1–0 but Palace chalked up a 2–0 win at Selhurst Park to make the final, going on to beat Blackburn over two legs to win promotion to the First Division. It was painful at the time but in hindsight the best team won. Steve Coppell and Palace had a great side at that time, with Mark Bright and Ian Wright making a formidable partnership up front. They each scored against us in the semi-final and Wright had a big hand in their final win against Rovers, showing the type of star quality anyone who had played against him knew all about at first hand.

Lou Macari had done tremendously to take Swindon that close to promotion to the First Division. Given his track record of taking the club through the divisions, it was no surprise when West Ham offered him the job at Upton Park. It was a good move from Lou's point of view and, given my struggles that season, a great move from my perspective.

It meant a fresh start and another chance to make a go of it with Swindon and make up for the most difficult year I ever had as a player. At every club before and after I was fortunate to be accepted by the fans and I fed off of their support, yet at the County Ground I hadn't done anything to catch their imagination. As far as they were concerned I hadn't lived up to the price tag – but I had a second chance to prove my worth.

7

OUT WITH THE OLD,
IN WITH THE NEW

Swindon has traditionally been a town more famous for the steam trains produced for the Great Western Railways than for football. You have to hand it to the powers that be at the County Ground though, they did their bit to put Town on the sporting map. When they lost Lou Macari, who had been a big appointment in his own right, the stakes were raised even further with the next name on the door of the manager's office.

Ossie Ardiles was a surprise choice, in the best possible way. He needed no introduction and had the type of playing CV that meant nobody could question him. He was untried as a manager but had the type of charisma and profile that suggested he would make a go of things at Swindon.

Ossie turned out to be a man of many talents. Aside from being a World Cup winner and (as it turned out) a top-class manager he was a qualified lawyer, chess master and international table tennis player. Mind you, I did whip him at darts – so he's got nothing to crow about!

It troubles me to now see Ossie throwing his hat in the ring for job after job and not getting a look in. In recent years I've seen him quoted expressing an interest in Caley Thistle and Aberdeen, amongst others. Presumably he's knocked on a few doors and I'm staggered none have opened for him. If I was a chairman, I'd take Ossie in a shot.

Maybe his easy-going personality has been his downfall to an extent, but behind the laughs and the jokes he's deadly serious about football. Maybe the fact that he's not from these shores counts against him – but Ossie speaks better English than plenty of people I know who have a British passport. He's spent long enough in the UK to qualify as one of our own.

But then again, I'm biased. Ossie Ardiles gave me the best year of my football life and I'll forever be in his debt for that. Playing under the great man was a revelation for me, like night and day after the season spent battling to fit into Lou Macari's masterplan.

Ossie was no sooner through the door at the start of the 1989/90 season than he ripped up that old blueprint and unveiled his take on the game. I wouldn't be so bold as to claim that we were the first team to play the diamond formation, but it certainly wasn't common when Ossie took it upon himself to put it into practice at Swindon.

We had a couple of former Spurs players on the books and they had told us that life with Ossie around would be anything but dull. They'd also told us we would love him to bits. They were right on every front.

The diamond was a joy for myself and Steve White to play in. The partnership I had with Steve was the best I ever encountered in my career, and I played with plenty of good forwards in my time. It's impossible to say exactly why it clicked for us, although my hunch is that it is because we were very similar characters. The old argument is that you want contrasting styles in a front pair, a big one and a little one or a poacher and a provider, but with Steve and me the opposite was true. We were both single-minded and out and out goal-scorers. It worked – we ended up with twenty-seven goals each, pretty much unheard of for a front two.

The onus on us as the front two in the diamond was to play as far apart from each other as we could, so it wasn't a conventional partnership. The logic was that by coming from wider areas and working the channels we were able to confuse the central defenders and pull them out of position. That left Alan McLoughlin, who would come through to play at the tip of the diamond, free to drive at the defence. Alan was perfect for that role and he went on to become a £1million player when he moved on to Southampton.

There was a big responsibility on the shoulders of David Kerslake and Paul Boden, the full-backs, to make the system work and they were able to get forward as much as they liked because of the security Colin Calderwood and Jon Gittens provided at the back. With Ross MacLaren, Tom Jones and Steven Foley in the middle of the park and Fraser Digby between the sticks it was a team with balance and a great blend of steel and silk.

There was a big turnover of players in the seasons after Lou Macari left the club and I think there had to be. I mean no disrespect when I say Lou's team had gone as far as it could. A lot of the players had come up with the club from the Fourth Division and to take the next step it needed something different, a new approach. Under Ossie, players like David Kerslake, signed from QPR, came in to bolster the squad and he also looked to the youth team, blooding Nicky Summerbee and Fitzroy Simpson amongst others that season. Both boys obviously had talent and went on to do well for themselves, Nicky notably with Manchester City and Fitz with Portsmouth. Years later I met up with Fitzroy in Scotland when he had a brief stint with Hearts – and it's fair to say the weather in the north wasn't totally to his liking. It wasn't a huge surprise when he cut short his time in Edinburgh and headed back south.

With fresh faces in the team, the fans certainly appreciated the change in style and in turn they grew to appreciate me.

Changing somebody's opinion of you is the hardest thing to do in life. Changing the opinions of a few thousand football supporters is even more difficult and doing that at the County Ground meant more to me than any medal. I went from being a player the Swindon fans would boo to their player of the year in the space of twelve months. That gave me a phenomenal sense of satisfaction and I'm glad I stuck around to put things right.

People often ask me what the highlight of my career was. Playing for Scotland was immense, cup finals with Aberdeen were memorable – but that season at Swindon under Ossie Ardiles must rank as the peak. Anyone who grew up watching Ossie at his best, as I had, knows that he was a magician of a football player. He was one of the finest of his generation, a truly world-class player, and I count myself very fortunate to have spent time working with somebody of his standing. He moved from a top-class player to a coach right out of the top drawer, even if he wasn't exactly one of the establishment in management.

Even the players who fell out of the team wouldn't have a bad word to say against Ossie. That tells you everything you need to know about the esteem he was held in by everyone who worked under him. The relationship between Ossie and the players was great. He wasn't a dictator in any shape or form, to the point of having a bottle of whisky on the dressing room table before matches. It was there for anyone who fancied a dram, but that was something I never did. Fraser Digby and Jon Gittens were two players who did make a point of taking a nip before kick-off, but the most would say no. It was the same on the Friday night before games. If the boys wanted a bottle of beer or glass of wine at the team hotel then Ossie was fine with that. Again, the most anyone would have was the odd shandy. Nobody abused Ossie's trust and I'm a great believer in letting individuals makes their own choices. Anyone worth their salt will not take advantage of a bit of freedom.

I only crossed that line once, and that was during Lou Macari's time. We went into the last game of the season with our place in the play-off secure and knowing we would play Crystal Palace in the semi-finals. We went to play Oldham at Boundary Park knowing that the result wouldn't have any impact on us at all and on the night before the game the mood at the hotel in Manchester was relaxed. The players decided to have a few beers – and a few beers turned into ten or fifteen. Lou found out about our little session the next day and he wasn't a happy man. He told us exactly how disappointed he was in us all. All except the full-back Dave Hockaday, who was tee-total. He may have been in Lou's good books, but it was Dave who sold one of the goals that day and he had an absolute nightmare. We weren't slow in suggesting he might try taking a few drinks before the next game.

In all seriousness, Dave was a good pro and one of the bunch who survived the transition between Lou and Ossie. That meant he was around for the roller-coaster ride that was Ossie's first season in management.

That 1989/90 campaign didn't start as well as we would have hoped, but then we were in the middle of a complete change in style and approach. We only won two of our first eight league games and were given a couple of real lessons, including a 4–0 up at Leeds.

Then it clicked for us. The next week we turned the tables, hammering Plymouth 3–0, and went on the run that took us all the way to the play-offs. We were scoring goals for fun and didn't look back. There were some absolutely cracking shows that season, with a 6–0 win at the County Ground against Stoke as well as a 4–3 at home to Blackburn. Wherever Swindon were involved, goals were guaranteed.

Those goals were shared right throughout the team, but the three of us at the top end of the diamond got the bulk. I hit twenty-five, Steve White grabbed twenty-three and Alan McLoughlin chipped in with sixteen of his own. During one purple patch in the middle of the season I got ten in ten games and we rapidly shifted up the table. We were briefly in the second automatic promotion place, but we had to settle for a play-off spot, a great achievement given the long list of big clubs in the division that year. West Ham, Wolves, Leicester and Middlesbrough were all among the teams below us and all would have bitten your hand off to get a place in the top six.

Leeds won the division, just beating Sheffield United to the punch, and left Newcastle, ourselves, Blackburn and Sunderland to fight it out in the play-offs. Newcastle, who had finished third, played Sunderland, in sixth, in the semi-finals and our reward for third place was a semi against Blackburn Rovers.

The previous season there had been a sense that we were fortunate to be in the play-offs. This time nobody was in any doubt that we deserved to be there – and that we deserved to go all the way and win. The semi-finals were both close-run affairs but we beat Blackburn 2–1 home and away to make it through to Wembley. Sunderland had edged out Newcastle to earn their place in the final and the stage was set.

We had an experienced side out that day. We lined up with Fraser Digby, David Kerslake, Paul Bodin, Alan McLoughlin, Colin Calderwood, Jon Gittens, Tommy Jones, myself, Steve White, Ross MacLaren and Steve Foley.

Sunderland had plenty of well known faces too. Gary Bennett was at the heart of their defence, always a tough opponent, Gary Owers and Paul Bracewell drove the midfield, and up front they had Marco Gabbiadini. Marco had been a prolific scorer for them over the years and was the main man again that season.

They had a good side – but we absolutely dominated them

that day. We must have had seventy per cent of the possession. The record books show we won 1–0, with Alan McLoughlin scoring the winner, but in truth it was far more convincing than that.

A few people had warned me that Wembley, with the scale of the pitch and the size of the crowd, could swallow you up if you weren't careful. They said to make sure I didn't let my energy get sapped too soon and I took that to heart, a bit too much as it happened. I turned to the referee to ask how long was left and couldn't believe it when he said there were twenty-five minutes to go. It had absolutely flown by. I was still feeling fresh as a button and thought I'd better get my backside in gear and start putting myself about a bit more.

There were near enough 73,000 people there that day and the sense of elation when the full-time whistle went was just incredible. The prize is so big in the play-off final that I'd say it eclipses any cup competition. The tension is impossible to describe but the relief when you win makes up for all of that. It's the most amazing experience, with an entire league season hinging on that one game.

On the day of the final, Michele was hundreds of miles away up in Aberdeen. The mother of a good friend had fallen into a coma and she had dashed to Scotland to be with them. Rather than Michele alongside me, I had two old friends from Fort William down for the big occasion. Norrie Bruce, a great mate of mine, and Angus Farmer, my best friend and best man, were at Wembley for the final – and back in Swindon for the celebrations that night.

By the time we woke up the next day it was 1pm and I'd missed the open-topped bus tour of the town. I've seen a video and it was an amazing day. Just about everyone in Swindon looked to be there to cheer the team. Everybody apart from me, since I was still in my bed.

There's a moment in the video when somebody shouted up to Chic Bates, who had stayed on as assistant manager after Lou Macari had moved on to West Ham, asking, 'Where's Shearer?' Chic, doing his best to be discreet, put his hand to one side of his face and mouthed: 'He's pissed.' When I look back, I'm gutted I missed that parade because it was a massive day for Swindon. The club had never been in the top division in more than 100 years of existence and I'd played a big part that season with so many goals to my name. I'm pretty sure if Michele rather than Norrie and Angus had been at home it would have had a different outcome, but at least we'd celebrated in style the night before. It was a momentous achievement to take a provincial club into the First Division, a true football fairytale.

8

FROM PENALTY BOX
TO WITNESS BOX

If the promotion success was a fairytale, the events that followed were a complete nightmare. Everything we had worked so hard to achieve began to unravel in front of us. To this day it remains one of football's greatest injustices that the players who beat the odds to win a place at England's top table never got the chance to savour the fruits of our labour.

After the joy and exhilaration of Wembley, Michele and I headed off for a quiet holiday on Jersey. It was there that I heard the bombshell news – Swindon Town had been relegated from the First Division before we had even kicked a ball at the start of the 1990/91 season. The incredible decision to kick us out of the top flight was the result of an investigation into irregular payments made to players at the County Ground. In their wisdom, the authorities decided not to knock us down just one tier but to put us down to the Third Division.

It was an absolute travesty, the most gut-wrenching experience I've had in the game. Here was me preparing myself for trips to Old Trafford and Anfield and then all of a sudden the rug was pulled from under my feet – it was the likes of Mansfield, Rotherham and Exeter we could look forward to playing against.

The punishment did not fit the crime. For the administrative mistakes made at boardroom level, a group of players who were more interested in football than money were being absolutely hammered. Yes, the club was being made to pay financially by missing out on the bounty of playing in the top league, but it was the players who were hurt most by the decision.

We were a small club and were being used as scapegoats. When Tottenham were dealt with for their financial irregularities in the early 1990s they were docked twelve points and given a hefty fine – a drop in the ocean compared to what we were hit with. I don't think any of the big clubs would have suffered in the same way; Swindon were an easy target.

On appeal, the decision was reduced to Swindon's relegation back to the Second Division rather than the third tier, but it was still a big kick in the teeth after everything we had done to win promotion in the first place. It was a nightmare for everyone who got caught up in the whole affair.

The first I knew about the financial suspicions surrounding the club was during a trip to St Austell in Cornwall. We were down to play against a local side but the action was all off the pitch. When we got up for breakfast we discovered that Colin Calderwood had been lifted by the police at the crack of dawn and taken back to London.

Colin was the spokesman for the players and the man charged with acting as a go-between. Because of that, he was the one who was in and out of the manager's office and involved in the negotiations over bonuses and all the rest.

When we discovered he was gone, we quickly found out what was going on. Colin had been taken in, questioned and then sent away again. Everything calmed down for a spell and we thought, or at least hoped, that we'd heard the last of it. Business carried on as normal at the club and we headed off to Spain for a few days of warm-weather training in Ronda.

All went to plan – until we got back on home soil. We touched down in London and were bussed back to the ground before heading our separate ways home by car. When I pulled up at the house there were two strangers parked outside and staring intently at the front door. Given that it was 10pm and a bit on the late side for visitors, it didn't take long to figure out that trouble was brewing. I hurried inside, locked the door behind me and sat down waiting for the door bell to ring. In fact it was the phone that went first. It was Ross MacLaren calling and he sounded more than a little bit agitated. Ross said: 'Duncan, is there someone parked outside your house?' I told him there was. He said: 'Whatever you do, don't let them in. They're from the Inland Revenue and I've got two of them sitting in my living room. They say they won't leave until I give them answers.'

Sure enough, there was a bang at the door. Being the big brave lad that I am, I went straight to the upstairs window to talk to them from there. They told me they wanted to come in and speak to me but I said there was no way I was letting them in at that time of night and that they would have to phone the club and make an appointment to see me. Reluctantly, they turned on their heels and I was spared the inquisition poor old Ross had to put up with. It was some welcome home.

The next day, when we arrived at the County Ground, we were taken straight into the boardroom by the chairman, Brian Hillier. He told us that if we all stuck together then nobody could touch us. A minute later, one of the boys looked out of the window and saw two minibuses full of suits pulling up out the front of the stadium. From that moment on it seemed less certain that nobody could touch us.

All of the office staff had been ordered out and every single document was systematically removed and taken away as evidence in the investigation. In front of our eyes, the colour drained from the chairman's face.

I've never been one to suffer too badly from pre-match nerves, no matter how big the crowd was. It was a different ball game standing up in front of a handful of people in the High Court, when the case finally reached its conclusion after a long investigation. The crux was that the club stood accused of tax evasion by making large cash payments to players outside of the normal Inland Revenue controls.

I was in the witness box with a pretty clear conscience, since the only cash payment I'd received was a £700 bonus, which we had all been promised after winning three matches on the bounce. In the scheme of things it was a tiny amount and I honestly never thought twice about the fact that it was cash in hand. It didn't seem that remarkable. The only thing I do have to declare about that payment is that I told Michele it was £500 and pocketed the other £200 for myself – I've just set the record straight.

The whole experience of being in court was an eye-opener, in more ways than one. The fine print of our contracts was being pawed over in public. I had signed at around the same time as Ross MacLaren had joined from Derby. He had cost £150,000 and I was a £250,000 signing. I remember at the time we'd briefly chatted about the contracts we had landed. Ross had told me he'd received the same signing-on fee as me – somewhere in the region of £20,000.

It so happened that I was up in court at the same sitting as Ross and my ears pricked up when the prosecutor turned to him and said, 'Mr MacLaren, you were paid a £35,000 signing fee by Swindon Town when you signed, in accordance with the terms of your contract.'

Ross looked at me, I looked at him and he didn't need to ask what I was thinking. I'd been well and truly stung with my fee and he'd done very nicely for himself. The last thing the club wanted was for the players to know the terms of each other's contracts – but that became the least of their worries.

The Inland Revenue, when I eventually agreed to speak to them, were pretty clear that they weren't coming after me or any of the players – in their words, there were 'bigger fish to fry'. They told me and the rest of the boys that the club would be responsible for any unpaid taxes on irregular payments – and some odd practices started coming out of the woodwork.

Even the groundsman became involved. He had been hauled in and quizzed over £25,000 of hay that he was supposed to have signed for. He was sure he hadn't, especially since there hadn't been any hay on the park for twenty-five years. That was just one of the weird things going on around the club at that time. All added together, it didn't make for a good case when it came to trying to persuade the football authorities not to come down too hard on us.

The irregular payment saga wasn't the only scandal to centre around the club. Lou Macari had been investigated over illegal betting after a wager of £4,000 had been placed on Swindon to lose an FA Cup game up at Newcastle. It was an insurance policy more than anything – if the team had won then the £4,000 would have been more than covered by the money earned in the next tie. If the team had lost, at least the expenses would have been covered by the return on the bet. It broke every rule in the book, but you could see why it appeared to make good business sense. Not surprisingly, it caused Lou a lot of grief – but nothing close to what the chairman faced at the end of the trial over the irregular payments.

Brian Hillier was jailed for a year later reduced on appeal and it was a horrible, horrible time for everyone at Swindon. The chairmanship changed a few times after that, but even the disappointment of relegation didn't shake the great spirit we had within the squad. The nucleus of the promotion-winning team stayed together and we regrouped for another crack at it.

The biggest loss was Ossie, who moved on to Newcastle

towards the end of the 1990/91 season. Again Swindon pulled off a massive coup when it came to replacing him – with Glenn Hoddle unveiled as the next big name at the County Ground.

Ossie landed up at Spurs before too long and it wasn't a big surprise when he came back for Colin Calderwood, who had been an absolute rock throughout my time at Swindon. I never once expected my phone to ring though. While I had been a good goal-scorer in the Second Division, in my heart of hearts I felt the top flight in England would have been a step too far for me. I didn't have the pace or the mobility you need to be a success at that level, something my new boss did his best to improve.

It was an honour and a privilege to work under Glenn Hoddle and to play on the same park as him. When he came in, he played at the heart of the team from the off, either in midfield or the centre or defence, and it was an incredible experience. He was a class apart from anyone I played with, his vision and passing ability simply sublime.

Glenn once said in an interview that I could volley a ball better than anyone he'd ever seen and I took that as a huge compliment, especially since it was something I'd always worked to perfect. To get recognition from somebody of his ability meant a lot to me.

He brought John Gorman in as his assistant and I got on very well with the pair of them. I found Glenn to be an absolute gent – he'd apologise if he swore in front of you. He was also an incredibly good coach and manager and it didn't surprise me one bit when he went on to land the England job. It was disappointing the way it worked out for him after that, to see his character attacked in the way it was.

With Glenn and Micky Hazard in the same team it was a striker's dream. Whatever run you made, the ball would land right in front of you. I thought the twenty-five goals in the promotion winning season was a respectable tally but under Glenn it got even better. I had equalled Don Rogers' post-war scoring record of thirty-two for Swindon when Blackburn came in for me and took me to Lancashire towards the end of the 1991/92 season. It's a big regret that I never managed to go one better and get the record for myself.

Training under Glenn was fantastic, with the ball involved in just about every session. Glenn had to change things around when he came in, primarily because the main man in the diamond formation was taken out of the equation.

When Alan McLoughlin was sold to Southampton it took a big cog out of the machine. He had been absolutely immense for us and Ian Branfoot at Southampton had watched him for months before landing him for a cool £1million. Then, having seen him star as the tip of the diamond, he contrived to play him wide left. Alan's experience was similar to the one I had during my first season at Swindon and the Southampton fans really didn't take to him, through no fault of his own.

With Alan removed from the team, we moved to a more conventional 4–4–2, with Glenn pulling the strings. The approach remained the same as it had been under Ossie, a total football approach.

I loved working under Glenn. I'd scored close to thirty goals the previous season but he was convinced he could squeeze more out of me. He would stay behind with me after training, keeping one of the goalkeepers to work with us, and spent hours hitting balls and perfecting my shooting. He also spent time with me to get me moving more off the ball and working harder on that side of the game. My philosophy had always been that any time and energy I spent chasing down full-backs or tackling back was taking me away from where I could do most damage – in and around the box. Glenn changed that attitude and it worked. I raced past the previous total and had my best ever haul for a single season. I thought surely this time it would have a happy ending, but didn't realise there was about to be a big twist in the tale.

9

LANCASHIRE HOT SHOT

At the start of the 1991/92 season there was only ever going to be one winner of the Second Division. Or so we were told. Blackburn Rovers had Jack Walker at the helm and he meant business. Jack had sold his steel business and started ploughing his millions into his hometown club. With Kenny Dalglish in charge, alongside his trusty lieutenants, Ray Harford and Tony Parks, and the not insignificant matter of Jack's money behind them, there was a real expectancy around Rovers going into that campaign.

They had invested heavily but wisely to put together a really talented squad of players. From Bobby Mimms in goal and Colin Hendry at the back, through to Tim Sherwood, Roy Wegerle and David Speedie, there was a brilliant group of players at the club. Everything was geared towards success – but they didn't have it all their own way. Far from walking away with the league, they had a fierce pack on their tails right the way to the end. It left Blackburn scrambling for a play-off place and when little old Swindon Town began to close in on them it really set the cat among the pigeons.

It wasn't until after I signed, with just months of that 1991/92 season to go, that I discovered the real fear wasn't about us catching them. It was about ending up in the play-offs with us again and having to try and get past us.

After defeating them home and away in the previous season's semi-final, we obviously had the beating of them. I used to love sitting chewing the fat with Ray Harford after I'd gone to Blackburn and he admitted to me that they just didn't know how to handle Swindon, particularly the way Ossie had us playing at that time. Ray was really curious about the system and how it worked. He was adamant that the one side they didn't want to face in the play-offs was Swindon.

It wasn't until Gordon Cowans piped up during one of those discussions that my suspicions were first aroused about the motivation behind recruiting me. Gordon turned and said: 'You know what they say about the cowboys and Indians. If they wanted to get the better of the Indians they had to take out the chief.'

That was it in a nutshell. I was Swindon's chief as far as Blackburn were concerned and they had dealt with the problem in the way only Blackburn could. Ray was too much of a gent to admit to it in as many words, but he didn't have to. The £750,000 they spent on me wasn't just about bringing in a player to cover for Mike Newell, who was out with a broken leg at that time, but just as much about weakening the main opposition for a promotion place.

I wasn't totally oblivious, mind you. When I first signed for Blackburn, I spoke to Michele pretty soon after and told her I didn't think we should start looking for a house in Lancashire. I said we should hang fire. Deep down I knew it was a short-term adventure and one I'd have to roll with as it developed.

Instead of upping sticks completely, I spent the week in a hotel in the North West, while Michele stayed at home in Swindon with our daughter Hayley, who was just two-and-a-half at the time. My gut instinct was that we wouldn't be putting down roots in Blackburn, despite the fact I'd just put my name to a two-and-a-half-year contract.

It wasn't easy to split up the family like that but we made the best of a difficult situation, with Michele coming up to stay every second weekend and me getting back down the road as often as I could.

I had to keep a low profile back in Swindon though. The whole affair had left a sour taste with the fans I'd left behind – although they were angrier with the club for selling me and Blackburn for engineering the situation than they were with me. I still read the local newspapers and there were letters every week from disgruntled supporters, who had cottoned onto the fact I'd played half a dozen games and then fallen out of the Blackburn team. In the meantime, Swindon's promotion challenge had faded away and they had fallen out of the play-off places. In the eyes of the Town faithful, Blackburn were a disgrace.

Everything was in a bit of a spin for the Shearer household at that time. One minute we were settled and happy in Swindon and the next we were getting ready to pack our bags – and it wasn't Blackburn that we expected to be moving to. Before I even knew Rovers were interested, I'd basically agreed to move to Notts County. All I had to do was give the final go-ahead and sign the contract at Meadow Lane.

It was Notts County who set the transfer merry-go-round spinning when they weighed in with a £500,000 offer. After the tax affair, Swindon weren't in a position to turn down an offer of that size for any player.

For the first time in my career I enlisted an agent, who had been recommended to me by my Swindon team-mate David Kerslake. It wasn't just any agent though, it was Eric Hall. To call Eric a character wouldn't be doing him justice – he's an incredible individual. When you consider he started his adult life at acting school and sang backing vocals for Tiny Tim in the 1960s, you get an idea that he wasn't exactly a typical businessman. Most people's abiding memories of Eric are his 'monster,

monster' catchphrase, his never-ending supply of cigars and the camp persona that he honed to perfection. He's hardly the shy and retiring type, as I discovered.

Initially he'd been an agent in show business, but he branched out into football in the 1980s and 1990s, signing up a string of big-name players and a lot of the London lads in particular. He didn't like to stray too far north and when I landed up in Aberdeen that must have tipped him over the edge. I remember him coming up for a meeting with me, getting off the plane at Dyce and taking me for lunch at the airport hotel before wishing me well and hopping back on a flight back to the safety of the Big Smoke – effing and blinding about Aberdeen and the Scottish weather as he disappeared through the departure gate. I might as well have signed for a team at the North Pole but by then he'd done his bit for me and he proved to be a shrewd operator.

As far as I know Eric's out of the football business altogether now, although I did hear him interviewed on the radio around the time of the 2010 World Cup. He was as brash as ever, as he did his best to wind up as many people as possible in space of a minute or two. The game could do with a few more big characters like him to liven things up a bit.

I'd never been convinced of the merits of using a middle man but I was persuaded to give Eric a chance and reluctantly gave it a go. He proved me wrong the day we went up to Nottingham for talks with Notts County. While the manager, Neil Warnock, and I talked football it was left for my new agent and the chairman Derek Purvis to talk numbers.

Notts County were in the top division but looked to be heading for relegation unless they could turns things around quickly. That was where I was supposed to come in. From the first offer they made me, my new agent squeezed them until we eventually settled on a wage two and a half times the initial figure I'd been quoted. It wasn't a bad day's work and I was glad I'd taken him with me.

The first time I met Eric was when he and his driver picked me up for the journey up to the Midlands. I wasn't exactly used to being chauffeured around, but I quickly discovered that Eric didn't do things by half and he liked the high life. On the road north he was promising me the earth, telling me we'd be able to get this and that out of County if we played our cards right. Even though they were playing in the big league at the time, I thought he was in cloud-cuckoo land with the type of figures he was bandying around. In actual fact he proved to be worth his weight in gold and wasn't wide of the mark with his expectations.

On top of the salary he managed to negotiate, there were other incentives built into the deal, depending on whether I could help keep County in the First Division and how many Scotland caps I won. As a twenty-nine-year-old who hadn't had a sniff of international football, that was the furthest thing from my mind.

It was typical of Eric though, always thinking a few steps ahead and trying to take a mile when he was given an inch. After all my terms had been thrashed out, he turned to the chairman and said, 'Now, let's talk about my fee.' Derek Purvis basically told him to take a hike, saying that he would never pay an agent a penny and that if anyone was going to be lining Eric's pocket then it would have to be yours truly. In actual fact, I'd already agreed a fee with Eric to broker the deal long before we'd pitched up at the stadium, deciding to pay him a flat figure rather than sign up to a contract promising him a percentage of my earnings. When he'd asked for a little extra finder's fee from the Notts County chairman he was obviously just trying to see how far he could push them and try to earn himself a nice little bonus. It was worth a shot, but his adversary was wise to him and he had to take no for an answer.

Agents get a lot of flak and have been blamed for all of football's financial woes at one stage or another. The bottom line is that they're only doing their job and watching Eric in full flow was like a masterclass in negotiation. It has always been for the clubs to be strong in the face of that type of pressure. It doesn't matter how good an agent is, if a team knows its limits and sticks to them then it will stay clear of trouble. Unfortunately too many have buckled in the face of outrageous demands and crippled themselves in the process.

As a player you can only take what is offered and it's fair to say that I felt the talks that day had gone in my favour, thanks in no small part to Eric's intervention on my behalf. After the finer details had been agreed, the chairman asked me what I was thinking. I said, 'The bottom line is that Swindon need to sell me. I'll be sad to leave but this is a chance to test myself at the top level and I want to play for Notts County.'

That was what he wanted to hear and we parted. I planned to go home, talk things over with Michele and get back to him the next day to dot the Is and cross the Ts. Although it would be a wrench to leave Wiltshire, the fact that my wages would more than double was a pretty persuasive argument. Michele had always been supportive of my career and was happy to go with my instinct, so we were all geared up to move to Nottingham.

I went to training the next day and chapped on Glenn Hoddle's door, ready to tell him my decision and thank him for everything he'd done for me. I walked in and he said: 'Before you speak, there's been a development.' I thought: 'Here we go, he's going to ask me to stay on.' Glenn said: 'Kenny Dalglish has been on the phone. He wants to speak to you.'

When you've grown up in Scotland with posters of Kenny Dalglish on your wall, there's no contest when he arrives on the scene. I arranged to meet up and went back to tell Glenn: 'I'm travelling up to Blackburn tonight to talk to them and, between you and me, that's who I'll be signing for.' My mind was made up before I knew the first thing about what they were offering or what they had planned for me.

It wouldn't have taken a genius to guess that was the way I would go and Glenn was resigned to it. He was furious, but he understood. Glenn didn't want to sell me, but his hands were tied. With the taxman desperate to make up for lost time, every penny was vital to keep Swindon afloat.

I rounded up my agent again, got on the road to Blackburn and had time to get back on the phone to Michele to keep her up to speed with what was happening. When I walked into Ewood Park the decision became even easier. The first person I bumped into was David Speedie, who I'd played with at Chelsea, followed pretty soon after by my good pal Colin Hendry. Next I saw Roy Wegerle, another of my old Stamford Bridge team-mates. If I didn't know better it could have been scripted to make me feel at home.

I met Kenny Dalglish and everything was agreed quickly. When you had the financial muscle of Blackburn, there wasn't too much haggling to be done. Blackburn structured their contracts like no other club I've ever dealt with. You agreed a contract length, came up with a figure to cover that period of time and then decided how you wanted it paid.

The choice was either a big signing-on fee and more modest wages or a big weekly wage coupled with a smaller signing-on fee. The sum of money being talked about for that two-and-a-half-year contract was beyond all my expectations and it was at that point that Kenny stepped in to give me a brilliant piece of advice. He asked me to come up with a figure for a weekly wage that would give us enough to get by on comfortably. I did that and he said, 'That's fine. We'll give you all the rest as lump sums.'

What that meant was that if I did move on before my contract expired, or more specifically if Blackburn sold me in that time, I would still get the package paid virtually in full. The clause in the contract was that as long as it was the club's decision to sell, they had to honour all of the signing-on fees agreed to.

When I moved to Aberdeen just months later, I received a very nice chunk of money from Blackburn because of Kenny's advice. If I had opted to take a huge weekly wage instead, I wouldn't have been entitled to a penny beyond my last week of work with them. Kenny knew fine well that I had been brought to the club to do a job, help get them out of the Second Division and then move on. With Alan Shearer already on his radar, there wasn't much scope for a long stay.

I'm very fortunate to have married a lovely woman who had the same mindset as me. Instead of rushing out to buy a fleet of fancy cars, we put it all away in a pension fund. We both appreciated that football was the only trade I knew and that it was a short career. The short time at Blackburn helped to set us up for later life and already that pension has proved to be a sensible investment and a big help with life after football.

It was an incredible period of transition for Blackburn. Ewood Park was nothing like the stadium as it stands now; it was still very much a Second Division ground. The team was also under development and that season Kenny used thirty-four players in the league alone as he tinkered to try and get the blend right.

There were a lot of familiar names on that squad list too. From Bobby Mimms in goal to Kevin Moran and David May at the back, Tim Sherwood in midfield and David Speedie up top. Other than Speedie, there were a lot of recognisable faces to Scottish supporters as well, with Lee Richardson involved and Colin Hendry having a big part to play.

Blackburn had led the Second Division for large chunks of the season by the time I joined. In the end there was a scrap just to stay in the play-off places, but it was the end result that was important rather than how we got there. Promotion was the be all and end all and they'd go to any length to get it.

The £750,000 spent to take me away from Swindon was a significant piece of business for Rovers. There was a big press conference to announce the signing and one of the first questions I was asked was if my family would be coming down for my debut. I told it like it was, making it clear that I didn't expect any relatives down from Fort William and that my grandad certainly wouldn't go to the game. Sensing they were onto a decent line, a Shearer family feud, the reporters pressed me further. Why wouldn't my grandad be watching me? I said: 'He's been dead twenty-five years.' It broke the ice in the press room and tickled Kenny too. Any time I've bumped into him since then he's always asked after my grandad.

Kenny may have been an absolute legend, but he was a genuine and down-to-earth character. In many ways, a perfect fit for Jack Walker. Jack lived away on Jersey as a tax exile and would come back as often as he could. Robert Coar, the chairman, ran the show in his absence, but it was Jack's drive and ambition that took Blackburn from the Second Division all the way to the Premier League crown.

Every single one of his players had the utmost respect for Jack. There was no question of him being some sort of cash cow. There was an understanding of what he wanted to achieve and the effort that went into training and playing reflected that. When we won the play-off at Wembley, there was clamour to get Jack down from the stands to join the celebrations – but he wasn't in it for the limelight or the attention; he wanted to see his dream come true. He was humble, despite his wealth, and I don't think he had ever lost sight of his working-class roots. It was a real fairytale because it was a club he loved, not just a plaything.

I loved being part of it and in the short time I was at Ewood I made some great friends and played with some wonderful talents. Gordon Cowans fell into both categories – he was probably the best footballer I played with, a phenomenal talent, yet underrated at the same time. He also had a great pair of lungs and could run all day – unlike his Scottish drinking buddies. After one night out, Speedie and I turned up for training feeling a bit woozy and struggling to get going. Gordon, who had matched us drink for drink, sailed past us as if he'd been tucked up in bed by nine o'clock.

There was a pretty relaxed attitude at Blackburn under Kenny, with time for work and play. My first real experience of that was a trip away to Dalmahoy for a golfing break with the squad. We stopped for lunch on the way up the road and watched back-to-back FA Cup semi-finals on the television. The first thing Speedie did when we arrived was order a round of pints . . . and they kept coming right the way through the 180 minutes of football. In between, Kenny was talking us through the games and it was an education to sit with him and get his take on the play. Mind you, I think the new boy was being used as a bit of a decoy – every time Kenny turned to speak to me, Speedie nipped away to order another round.

The next morning we were up at 8.30am for golf at Dalmahoy. We came in for lunch and then Kenny and a few of the boys headed back out for another eighteen holes. They came back in, then Kenny went back out for another nine holes. It was then you realised why our team-building weekend was at a golf course. The man is just addicted to the game.

I wasn't there long enough to learn everything I could have from Kenny, but even in the few sessions I did have on the training field with him I became a better player.

He worked with me on holding up play, teaching me to stick my backside into defenders and really make a nuisance of myself, and even playing alongside him in five-a-side games was an experience. He hadn't long finished playing and was still fit as a fiddle and still had the touches. He was also a real nark if things didn't go his way – a stray pass or a bad touch and he was on you like a ton of bricks, even in training games.

He had met his match in David Speedie though – the two of them would fight like cat and dog. One week, when David had just come back from suspension, they had a real stramash. Speedie was ordered into Kenny's office. Then minutes later I was ordered in after him. Kenny said: 'I'm putting that little shit Speedie on the bench. You'll be taking his place.'

I said, 'Not a problem, boss.'

Kenny hit back with: 'It is a problem. I hate leaving him out – but he's a moaning wee bastard and needs to be taught a lesson.'

When I joined Blackburn, I had been put up by the club in a hotel with Roy Wegerle and Tim Sherwood. Then Mr Speedie would come up from London midway through the week and wreak havoc. Speedie was a manager's nightmare but a great character. My first real experience of him was walking back from training at Chelsea's old Harlington ground by Heathrow and catching snippets of an argument going on behind me between wee David and big Joe McLaughlin. I heard Joe having a pop at David's passing and Speedie sniping back, saying he was too busy picking Joe's balls out of Row Z to play any balls of his own. The next thing I heard was a slap, then a thud. I turned round to see David laid out on the deck. Joe had settled that little debate.

I used to share a car with Big Joe and Derek Johnstone when I was at Chelsea. Without fail, the conversation would turn to food when those two got together and they were brilliant company. Never mind playing football, they could eat for Scotland. D.J.'s a top man – not just a great player but a wonderful character.

Speedie and my fellow hotel-mate Roy Wegerle made life away from the family in Blackburn a little easier than it would have been if I'd been on my own. I had played with Roy at Chelsea and I can picture his introduction to the English game as if it was yesterday. It was in a reserve game against Arsenal, who had Pat Jennings between the sticks. Roy picked up the ball in midfield and set off on a run that produced the best individual goal I've ever seen. We were all left standing staring at each other, wondering who on earth this guy was. He'd come in from college football in America and you could see from that one piece of brilliance that he had a big future in front of him.

While Roy became a main man at Blackburn, I had to adjust to a different role. It was a bit strange for me to face up to life as a substitute, being drafted in here and there. Ever since leaving Chelsea I'd been a first-choice striker and it wasn't nice to be back on the bench. There was no way I was going to make a fuss, though. I knew my place and that was as part of a squad for that crucial part of the season.

We lost on my debut, going down 2–1 to Barnsley despite me getting my traditional first-game goal, but I played in the next five of the eight games in the run to the end of the season. Having led the league at one stage, it was a case of clinging on to sixth place to earn a place in the play-offs by the end of a nervous season.

I kept my place in the side for the first leg of the play-off semi-final, when we ran over the top of Derby County and beat them 4–2. By the time we edged through to the final, losing 2–1 but winning 5–4 on aggregate, I had dropped out of the side and was in the stand for the final against Leicester. Mike Newell, who had taken my place when he came back from injury, scored the penalty that proved to be the difference between the sides.

I was part of another promotion party at Wembley but yet again it looked as though I wouldn't get the reward of playing in the top flight at the end of it. I had a feeling that my brief time at Ewood Park was coming to an end and the hunch turned out to be right.

10

THIRD TIME LUCKY

Aberdeen had wanted me when I had first been on trial in the early 1980s, but my decision not to travel south for a second training stint scuppered that move. Aberdeen had wanted me when I was on hot scoring form with Swindon in the early 1990s, but on that occasion it was Jack Walker's cheque book that put paid to their plans to take me to Pittodrie. It was in the summer of 1992, a decade after I had first come close to signing, that I finally made it to Aberdeen at the third attempt.

Before I went to Blackburn in March 1992 there had been interest from Willie Miller at the Dons. As soon as he found out Rovers were interested, Aberdeen dropped out straight away. Nobody in the land could compete when Blackburn came on the scene, but things had changed quickly for me at Ewood Park and it was Willie who was first to react.

At the end of the 1991/92 season, after just three months in Lancashire, I got a call from Kenny Dalglish before he headed off on his holidays. He said: 'Duncan, there's a new contract sitting waiting for you and every other player who helped us up to the Premiership. You can sign it and stay and fight for your place – or I am prepared to let you speak to Aberdeen. They've come in for you and I thought you might be interested.'

He was right – I was more than interested. After so long away from home it was a chance to get back to Scotland – and Aberdeen had been such a massive club when I was growing up. Given that it was a city Michele had already spent a bit of time in, everything about it felt right.

As soon as I got the call, it all moved very quickly. Eric Hall flew up to Scotland to handle the negotiations and although there was the usual bartering it was actually an easy deal to strike. I had my lump sum from Blackburn due to me and Aberdeen knew that, so they tried to negotiate a package that didn't include a signing-on fee. Eric, in his inimitable style, soon put them straight on that and without any real hesitation Willie Miller put together a contract that was attractive enough to make it happen. I knew what was on the table was Aberdeen's best offer and it was a challenge that excited me more than money ever would. No doubt Mr Hall would have been happy to have really gone in for the kill but I wanted it done quickly and that's what happened.

My only problem was that the move came slap bang in the middle of my summer holidays. My habit was to spend a month of the close season eating, drinking and relaxing. Then, a couple of weeks before pre-season, I'd get myself into shape ready for the hard work of training.

Because the Scottish and English seasons were out of sync, I pitched up at Pittodrie weeks behind the rest of the Aberdeen players, who had already started pre-season. I was carrying a fair bit of extra weight and ended up doing extra sessions with Drew Jarvie to try and get my fitness built up. It was far from ideal, but Drew put me through my paces and I was able to shift the pounds I needed to catch up with the rest of the boys.

At £500,000, the fee was a big one for Aberdeen to pay and it was just as big a thing for me to turn my back on Blackburn – the club and the bonuses. We were on £300 a point and that meant plenty of £900 win bonuses during that promotion-winning season. We were earning more in bonuses alone than a lot of players were collecting in wages.

At the same time, I knew if I wanted regular football I had to move on. As you would expect, there was an influx of players at Blackburn in time for the first season of the Premiership. Henning Berg and Graeme Le Saux were brought in to give options at the back and the attacking side of the team wasn't neglected. Alan Shearer was obviously the key signing but there were others brought in at the same time; Jason Wilcox, Stuart Ripley and Kevin Gallacher also had a major impact.

I left all that behind because I had a great feeling about Aberdeen. David Wylie, the physiotherapist, picked me up at the airport and I doubt he was expecting the reaction he got when he told me that the club wasn't going away on tour for pre-season. It was the first time in ages there hadn't been a trip, with Alex Smith favouring Holland for his preparations before Willie Miller took over. Instead of a foreign training camp, the decision had been taken to stay close to home and take on Highland League clubs. I'm sure there were a few long faces when that announcement was made, but for me it was brilliant news. I'd left the Highland League a decade before and it felt like a lifetime. To be heading back to some of my old stomping grounds was great fun.

I roomed with Alex McLeish during that little tour of the north and it started to dawn on me what it meant to play for Aberdeen when I was sitting there with a man who has seen it all, done it all and won it all. Having people like Alex around the club meant there were always reminders of what we were striving for – the standards that had been set during the glory days. To me, that's no bad thing.

Big Alex had been part of the squad when I'd been down on trial in the early 1980s and there were plenty of other familiar faces still involved when I finally made it onto the Pittodrie staff.

I loved to chew the fat with Teddy Scott in his incredible kit room, the most glorious corner of any football ground I've ever visited. The key was to make sure you had plenty of time to spare because Teddy could keep you talking for hours.

I mentioned before that I'd had fun pulling Teddy's leg about the decision not to sign me while I was still with Clach, but it turned out that they had been watching me far more closely than I ever knew. I had assumed that when the trial didn't go to plan all those years ago Aberdeen's interest ended, when in fact the chief scout Jimmy Carswell had followed my career closely. Teddy dug into one of his cabinets, where he had everything perfectly filed, and pulled out one of Jimmy's reports from my Huddersfield days. Jimmy had commented: 'Duncan Shearer is big, strong, has an eye for goal, is Scottish and from our area – this is a player we must have at Pittodrie.' It's strange reading things about yourself, especially when you've got no idea all of that is going on behind the scenes. They never did act on that recommendation, although there were murmurs during Ian Porterfield's time in charge that Aberdeen might make a bid. At around the same time there were reports of interest from Jim McLean at Dundee United, but it wasn't until I'd really proved myself in England that I got the chance in the Premier Division.

To get that chance with Aberdeen was fantastic. My best mate Angus 'Og' Farmer was a key man with the Fort William branch of the Dons supporters' club. They'd make the four-hour bus journey across for just about every home game and I'd grown up knowing just how big Aberdeen Football Club was right the way across Scotland. The Old Firm had supporters' clubs in the Fort too, but the strength of feeling for Aberdeen throughout the Highlands was phenomenal. The fact that buses would snake their way across to Pittodrie from even the most remote areas tells you everything about how devoted the fans were and still are. It's a sign of the times that I now see familiar faces who used to be in the stands at Pittodrie now watching Ross County and Caley Thistle, but there's still plenty of support in the north and west for the club.

For the time I was at Pittodrie I brought a little bit of Lochaber to the Granite City. Eoin Jess thought I was pulling his leg when I pointed to the big framed print of the landscape from Loch Linhe up to Ben Nevis that he had received from the Fort William supporters' club and said, 'That's the house I was born in.' I still don't know if he believed me in the end, but sure enough there was the family home. It was 160 miles away on the other side of the country, but it was still Dons country.

Now I found myself on the east coast and really embedded in Aberdeen life. I was put up by the club at the Thistle Hotel in Altens while I found my feet, lodging there along with Roy Aitken after he had moved up to become Willie's assistant, and before long we found a house on Gray Street in the west end of the city and settled quickly. I was out building a slide in the garden for Hayley one afternoon when the phone rang inside and Michele picked it up. She shouted out: 'That's Kenny some-body on the phone for you.' Of course it was Kenny Dalglish, on to wish me well. I came off the phone saying: 'The next time he calls you better bow down. That's the King you just called "Kenny somebody or other". It's easy to see you're English.'

Michele was never a big football aficionado and very rarely came to watch me play. She'd had a bad experience at Swindon during my difficult first season there, listening to the crowd jeering at me, and that put her off. It hurt her more than it hurt me and we agreed afterwards that it was better to pick and choose the games she came along to. Fortunately my days of being barracked by crowds were in the dim and distant past and from day one at Pittodrie I had wonderful backing from the fans.

11

LIKE FATHER, LIKE SON

The move back to Scotland brought me right back into the thick of the action. By that I don't mean nightclubs or parties – that was never my scene. For me, being in the thick of it meant two completely different things: hunting and fishing. I can only imagine what some of the tabloids would have made of it if they'd seen me, the Scotland striker, sneaking around in the dead of night, landing catches on the sly and trying my best not to get collared. It was a very different type of poaching from the kind most footballers specialised in.

For me it was second nature, though. My dad, Duncan senior, worked for a few construction companies when I was younger and my birth certificate says he was a lorry-driver by trade – but I remember being asked his occupation for a profile in the Chelsea programme not long after I'd moved to London and I put him down as a retired poacher. It wasn't too far from the truth, since hunting and fishing were his real passions.

I can still remember waking up and going through to the kitchen to find half a dozen beautiful fresh salmon lined up on the stone and it wasn't unheard of to open the shed and find a stag being prepared for the pot. We ate like kings – although it was a case of fur coat and no knickers in some respects, because it was hard for him and Mum to support such a big family.

In later years I loved to sit having a few drams with Dad and his friends, listening to his tales and stories of his adventures. He would never take us kids out on his poaching trips but we did inherit his love of the outdoors and, like father like son, I'm still a keen fisherman to this day. We didn't go on holidays but the summers were glorious, spending all day every day at the water's edge trying to land a catch.

By the time I signed for the Dons I'd been away from it all for years, only getting back from England for summer holidays. In Aberdeen, I was just a three-and-a-half-hour drive from the west coast. With young children, it wasn't a case of travelling back and forth every week, but we would nip across as often as we could and it made it easier for friends to travel across to visit.

Wherever I've been in Britain, the west coast has always been where I've classed as home. I grew up in a house on Erracht Drive in Caol, on the edge of Fort William. We looked out over Loch Linnhe and had the best of Scotland's scenery all around us. It was a noisy and busy house, a family of nine. I was one of seven children, with big brothers William and David as well as my older sisters Katherine and Alison. Finlay – known as Midge – and Amanda were my juniors and we kept our parents on their toes.

Dad was born and bred in the area while Mum, Irene Flett Shearer, was from Kirkwall on Orkney. One of my proudest achievements was going to the island to collect the player of the year award from Orkney branch of the Aberdeen supporters' club in 1994. It was the first time I'd ever been and because of my mother's links to the area it was a special trip for me.

A lot of players would begrudge attending functions like those, especially when they were as far-flung as that, but for me it was always a pleasure. While others would sit and drink a couple of orange juices, playing the model professional, I'd have a few vodkas with the guys and make a night of it.

I'd been promised a warm welcome in Orkney and Marcus Shearer, who helped organise my visit on behalf of the supporters' club, told me I'd be in for a peaceful stay. He couldn't have been more wrong. When I arrived at the airport in Kirkwall I found myself being questioned by the police, who were investigating the now notorious murder of the waiter Shamsuddin Mahmood the night before I arrived. Here was me expecting some tranquil island scene and instead I walked into tales of somebody being shot in the head.

Police aside, the welcome I received was something else. They had given the children at one of the local schools time off to come out to cheer and wave scarves. They were lined up waiting for me and it was a brilliant gesture. I was taken on a tour of some of the island's sights and then had a great night at the presentation dinner, where I was presented with a Bride's Cog. The cog is like an open barrel that traditionally was filled with a potion and passed round at Orcadian weddings and I've still got that in my cabinet at home. Maybe it was the welcome I received, or the fact that it was my Mum's birthplace, but I fell in love with the place and I've been back several times since.

My mum had come across to the mainland as a young woman and worked as a legal secretary, doing her best to keep us all fed and watered. It was tough, though, and Mum would try and hide the bills from Dad when they were struggling to pay them, even when they were piling up. She took a lot on her own shoulders and I'll never forget the time the man came round to cut off the electricity. His name was Sandy McGonagall and my brothers and I still see him around Fort William – we're not slow in reminding him what he did to us. He was only doing his job, right enough, but it doesn't stop us from winding him up. It was difficult to live like that, more so for Mum than it was for us kids. We saw it as a bit of a game. It didn't seem like we were missing out on too much but we knew we weren't well off.

One thing's for sure – I've appreciated the finer things in life all the more because I know what it's like to make do with very little. We try and drum into the young players just what a wonderful life football can provide for you, but maybe you have to have been on the other side of the fence to appreciate that good fortune. I'd like to think I always kept my feet on the ground, and coming from a modest but happy family gave me a good base to build from. I'm pretty sure I never once lost sight of who I am or where I came from. I've always been proud of my roots.

Everything we did was outdoors, from fishing to football and shinty. Dad was a great shinty player in his heyday and won a lot of trophies and medals with Kilmallie. I loved the sport and still do – although the fact that I ended up playing for Lochaber didn't go down too well with Dad's mates, who gave me a fair bit of stick about that.

I still love to swing the caman when I can and I got back on the pitch in 2010, when our old Lochaber under-seventeen team was reunited to play against the current youth team. It was interesting to say the least – me with my hip replacement and a few bellies bigger than I remember them from back in the 1970s. We got off to a flyer, one up after the first minute, but got well and truly whipped 8–1 in the end. The young boys taught us a lesson that day, but we had a hell of a team when we were their age, winning quite a few cups and the league at that level. When Ally Ferguson called me up to get the boots on again I didn't think twice. It was a chance to roll back the years.

From the under-seventeens, I moved up to the Lochaber second team. In those days, because most people didn't have a phone in the house, you had to wait for a little card to drop through your letterbox on a Friday night to tell you if you had been picked for the first team or second string and where to report for duty. I came close to getting the big call-up. I'd badgered them after a good run of form, so I was sure I'd made it to the top team. I should have known better when Donnie McKenzie, the man with the cards in his hand, tried to slip the card breaking the news through the door quietly. I chased his car down the street trying to change his mind, cursing him under my breath, but it was no good.

I was fortunate to play in cup finals and for Scotland at football but my one regret is that I never made it to a Camanachd Cup final as a shinty player. I've been to plenty as a spectator, even doing co-commentary with Alison Walker for the BBC's television coverage at some of them, but I'd have given anything to have got the chance to get out there on the park.

In fact, I gave up my first ever Scotland cap to get my hands on a Camanachd Cup Winner's medal. Eck Sutherland, who grew up in the same street and was a good friend of mine, went on to star for Kingussie and win the cup. Years later he called into my house in Aberdeen. We got talking and eventually struck a deal to swap my first cap for his Camanachd Cup medal. I've still got it in pride of place along with my collection.

I at least had a little bit of experience with the caman. Caol was a school known as having a good football side but we were no pushovers in the shinty either. We reached the Mackay Cup final and played Skye and Portree – a team from a real shinty heartland. Needless to say we got whacked by them in that final.

Like everything else in sport, the game's changed a lot over the years. It has always been fast and furious but it's a lot safer now than it's ever been – with far more players wearing head-guards and a few new rules to keep people in check. I played centre-side and scored a good few goals. The beauty is you don't have to be too close to score.

Although we were well schooled in shinty through my dad's love of the sport, it didn't take long before football began to dominate family life. It was 1979 when John Neil signed my brother David for Middlesbrough. I was sixteen when he started out, but I never had it at the back of my mind that I could be, or even wanted to be, a footballer myself. The only thought I had was to get through school and find myself a good, steady job. It was difficult for Mum when her eldest started to fly the nest – but for us it meant there was two to a bed instead of three. We knew we'd still see plenty of him and we were all excited for him when he headed south.

By then we had shifted house to Glenkingie Street, still in Caol. It is still the family home now, with my brother Finlay in the house. It is on the banks of the Caledonian Canal, which was busy then with fishing boats making their way from the west coast through to Inverness. There would often be seven or eight boats tied up waiting to head up the canal and while the fishermen were taking a refreshment or two in the pubs, David spotted a golden opportunity for us to acquire some nets for the goals we used in the park. There was a fair bit of hullabaloo when they got back to their boat to find thousands of pounds' worth of net missing. It all ended with the police knocking at the door and David having to hold his hands up. They got them back . . . eventually.

Looking back, it's amazing how many scrapes we got into – and managed to get ourselves out of too. One way or another, we were lucky to survive long enough to play football at all.

There was one occasion when David almost hanged himself in a freak accident with the cord on his pyjamas. My sister Alison was heading downstairs to catch the ice cream van and had to pass the landing on the way, where David had been playing. I heard her telling Dave to stop messing around. But he wasn't kidding on – he was gone, he'd stopped breathing. The cord had got tangled round the banister and David was hanging there, his face was so blue he looked like something out of *Braveheart*. There was a big commotion and I was sent out of the house while someone else dashed across the road for help.

Our neighbour Margaret Buchanan was a nurse and she worked wonders that day, bringing David back to life when I think everyone else thought it was too late. She revived him once but he slipped away again. She managed to get him breathing a second time but again he passed out. She must have known her third attempt would probably be the last and fortunately for us it worked. His heart started pumping and he was out of danger. He was a lucky, lucky boy to survive and it was a terrifying experience for us all. It also ruined *Braveheart* for me – I can't watch the film without thinking of David dangling there. It was Mrs Buchanan's turn to be a hero, since her husband Jack already was – as a marvellous shinty goalkeeper for Fort William – and there were big headlines in the local papers about her role that day. They also played on the fact the ice cream van had probably saved David's life. I suppose that if it hadn't turned up at the right time and caught Alison's attention then he wouldn't be here today. Mind you, there are some people in Fort William who might say she should have left him hanging there. A bit harsh, I'd say.

I count myself fortunate to be here to tell the tale, after my own little brush with death. It was a few years after the fright we had with David when I had a similar experience. I was just twelve or thirteen and fishing with friends at the Corpach pier, grappling with a hook on a rope for tobies in among the seaweed. We'd go down underneath the pier – but this time there was a splash and I was taking a closer look than I'd expected, up to my eyes in water and being pulled out to sea by the current. I couldn't swim back then and I was in real trouble, slashing my hands as I tried to get a grip on the mussels that were clinging to the timbers of the pier. It was hopeless, though. I was getting dragged away and gulping down water as it went over my head. My mates on the pier were frozen with fear and it wasn't until a man who lived opposite the pier, Robert Payne, jumped in to save me that the nightmare was over. If it hadn't been for him, I'd be dead. My big brother Willie was with me that day and got the fright of his life, and he kicked my arse all the way up the road. Needless to say, swimming lessons were at the top of the agenda after that.

Despite all of our close shaves, we outlived our parents. Mum was just fifty-two when she died in 1983 – far too young. Dad passed away more than sixteen years later, early in 2000. Hogmanay had always been a big celebration for our family. It would go on for two or three days, with Dad going first-footing round all of his friends and neighbours. The year he died he didn't get up from his bed for it – he just didn't have the strength – and I knew then he was in a bad way. It just wasn't like him to miss out on New Year and sure enough he was admitted to hospital soon after. He was typical old school and refused to go and see a doctor in the days leading up to that, even though he was coughing up blood and desperately trying to hide from us how ill he was. Eventually we persuaded him to let the doctor come to the house and he only needed to take one look at Dad to decide he had to go to hospital. He was diagnosed with cancer and was too far gone for chemotherapy or radiotherapy to have any chance of working. Within four or five days he had passed away.

Again it was a really rough time for young Amanda, but also for Midgie. He and William were now alone in the big old house that had once been so alive with all the noise and mischief of seven children and my parents trying to keep us all in check. He's still there now, living with his girlfriend, and when you visit the house you still expect to hear the bedlam that there used to be when we were all running around the place. It feels a little empty, but the memories are still all around – like battling to be the middle one of the three in the bed during the freezing winters; or the smell of the meat Dad had caught cooking on the stove.

We're not a touchy-feely family, never have been. No matter how long I've gone without seeing my brother, I'm more likely to give him a wee nod of the head than shake his hand or give him a hug. It's the same with my sisters, and as long as I can remember it has always been that way. It doesn't mean we feel any less about each other; it's just the way we've always been.

My dad was very much a closed book through everything that happened to William and the loss of my mother. We knew he was hurting, but he never once opened up about how he was feeling. That was just his nature.

Mum died before I made my breakthrough in football and it's a big regret that she never got to see me play or share the good times that I had in the game. The last she knew was that another one of her kids had flown the nest and left her. She'd seen her daughters move on and away. Now it was another of her sons – she probably felt her whole world was collapsing around her.

My dad at least did get to see me make something of myself, although he never ever ventured away from Fort William to see me play. He did watch on television and I know he was proud to see me pull on the Scotland shirt – not that he'd give too much away. In fact, when I came home to see him he'd more often than not greet me by asking, 'When are you giving up that poofy game and going back to the shinty?'

I'd just say, 'That poofy game just bought you another forty-ouncer.' He couldn't argue with that. Every time I came back for the summer I'd take him a different type of whisky, a big forty-ounce bottle, and we'd spend the evenings sharing a few drams and telling stories. I treasured those times together – they were my holidays. I never wanted to go away to Majorca or Benidorm with the rest of the football set. To be back home with my dad, my family and my mates was all I ever wanted. Now my Mum, Dad and brother are all in the same graveyard at Kilmallie. There are few more beautiful places in the world to look out over when the sun is shining.

In a sense, the experience of Dad's death gave us an indication of what to expect when we discovered Willie also had cancer in February, 2005. What we didn't realise, though, was that people who have been paralysed do not have the ability to fight the disease. He was rushed up to hospital in Inverness, by which time my wife and I were back living in the city.

It was surreal to see how quickly he deteriorated. I've never seen anything like it in my life. One of his great friends, Robert 'Bunner' McGilvray, is a paramedic in Fort William and it was Bunner who drove Willie through to Inverness. We had grown up just a few houses apart in Caol and it hurt him to see how ill Willie was. Within hours of arriving he had passed away.

12

ABERDEEN AMBITION

It didn't take too long for me to realise that I hadn't just joined a football team when I was transferred to Aberdeen in 1992. I had signed up to become part of a cause. In Willie Miller there was a manager who had his sights set on taking the club back to the top of the tree and his motivation revolved around more than just what happened on the park.

From the first meeting I had with Willie – over a spot of lunch at the ground when I'd turned up with Michele to get everything signed and sealed – I got a sense of how much it meant to him to make a go of it. He had taken over from Alex Smith in February that year, so was still brand new to management.

Alex had been successful and left behind a talented group of players, but Willie was determined to take it to another level. After running Rangers so close on so many occasions under Alex, the next step was to win the championship. To do that he had to be bold and started rebuilding, on the back of the disappointment of finishing sixth at the end of the 1991/92 season.

Willie spent big to take me from Blackburn and – having splashed out more than £400,000 on Mixu Paatelainen from Dundee United just a few months earlier – he was pinning his hopes on a new-look £1million strike force. Hans Gillhaus, still at that stage the record signing at £650,000, had fallen out of favour after the change in management. The switch to a pairing of Mixu and me represented a new direction.

Scoring had been the big problem before we arrived, with just ten goals in the last fifteen games of the 1991/92 campaign and Eoin Jess leading the way with twelve goals for the whole season, despite not being an out-and-out striker. The board opened the cheque book to put that right. With Scott Booth and Eoin already on the scene, as well as experience and quality with the likes of Jim Bett pulling the strings in midfield, there was a good squad coming together.

From our first meeting, the manager made it clear that second best was not going to be good enough. It didn't matter how much money Rangers were throwing at their team, he believed we could get the better of them.

Willie also spoke about the west-coast bias and how we were up against it at Aberdeen. If I needed any convincing of how strongly he felt about that, I got it just a few weeks into pre-season training. A photographer arrived to do some promotional shots for the Panini sticker album and he had brought with him a huge background. It had images of players from Rangers, Celtic, Hearts, Hibs and a few others . . . but not a single Aberdeen player. A few of the other players and I had been picked out to be in the pictures and were getting ready for the photographer when Willie came striding over, demanding to know why there were none of his players on the promotional board. The poor photographer didn't know what had hit him and was sent away with a few choice words and his tail between his legs.

That was the first time I was really aware of the strength of feeling, but there were plenty of other instances. Halfway through my first season I won the Premier Division player of the month award, sponsored in those days by McEwan's. I got a lovely big wooden trophy, a carving of the McEwan's figure. I had my photos taken with it and the next day Willie pulled me into his office. On the desk was a copy of the *Daily Record* and he flicked from the back page, skipping a couple of pages before resting on the one where the photo and few paragraphs of text about my award were placed. It was there in black and white. Then Willie went into his drawer and pulled out a copy of the *Record* from months earlier, when Ian Durrant had won the same award. There was Ian on the back page of the paper in glorious colour, turning to a half-page feature on the inside page. Willie said: 'This is what you get when you're an Aberdeen player.'

That was when I really realised it was about more than just playing for Aberdeen Football Club – it was about still paying the price for what Willie and the rest of Alex Ferguson's side had done to the Old Firm all those years ago. Maybe I wouldn't have paid too much attention to it if it hadn't been pointed out to me, but from then on I began to notice little bits and pieces that did point towards a bias, maybe even resentment from certain quarters, when it came to Aberdeen. The siege mentality had worked for Sir Alex in the 1980s and I think Willie hoped to replicate that with the 1990s squad.

In my first season as an Aberdeen player, the 1992/93 campaign, we were so close yet so far from rolling back the years. The record books show we were runners-up in all three competitions to Rangers. With a few twists of luck in the right places, we could well have ended up as treble winners.

After being thrown into pre-season training earlier than I expected or would have hoped, I managed to get myself back in shape in time for the big kick-off. Hibs at home was the opening fixture and I was desperate to get myself off to a good start in front of the Aberdeen supporters. That meant I needed a goal.

It was a typical early season game in the first half, with both sides determined not to give anything away. We went in at half-time locked at 0–0, but after the break it burst into life. I scored twice and Scott Booth got another to give us a comfortable three-goal cushion by the end of play. It was mission accomplished on both fronts, for the team and its new striker.

It was an attack-minded side that started the season, with myself as well as Mixu Paatelainen and Scott Booth starting the match and Eoin Jess introduced from the bench. We were feeding off the good work of Paul Mason and Jim Bett in midfield. The defensive side was hardly lacking either, with Theo Snelders in his prime and the young talents of Gary Smith and Stephen Wright starting the season alongside the experience of Brian Irvine and David Winnie.

We had flair, but there was also strength in that side. For a start we had Roy Aitken, 'The Bear'. I'd played against Big Roy during my Swindon days, when he was at Newcastle, and knew how much of an influence he would have at Aberdeen. He was at the end of his playing career when he came up to be Willie's assistant, but he could still play the game and had the benefit of years of experience.

Then there was Mixu. When I scored the second of my two goals against Hibs, I turned to celebrate – and ran straight into Mixu. It was like colliding with a redwood tree, he was so solid. If ever there was a perfect physique for a football player, I would say Mixu had it.

As the season progressed Alex McLeish came back from injury while Stewart McKimmie and Brian Grant added their experience. Willie continued to tinker with the squad, buying Lee Richardson from my old club Blackburn and picking up what turned out to be a bargain. I think he'd first stumbled across Lee when he came to watch me at Ewood and was rightly impressed by what he saw.

It was a great team in so many ways, and well equipped to fight the Old Firm's fire with fire. We ended the season with me hitting twenty-eight goals and three others pushing twenty each. Figures like that were phenomenal and showed the variety in the play and the threat we carried from all angles. Mixu Paatelainen finished on twenty while Scott Booth was on nineteen and Eoin Jess on sixteen. Now most SPL managers would give their right arm for one striker capable of scoring fifteen or twenty goals a season. That year we had four. The expectation was for us to finish third but we managed to split the big two, overtaking Celtic and chasing Rangers hard in the league and cups.

For me the start of the season was vital. I always knew that getting off to a scoring start was vital after joining a new club. The Aberdeen fans didn't know Duncan Shearer, they didn't know what I was about. All they knew was my record from my last couple of clubs and what I had to do was show them that I had something to offer.

When the first goal against Hibs hit the back of the net it was a huge adrenalin rush. The goal wasn't spectacular, but as the first for the club it was so important. I can still picture it as if it was yesterday – Scott Booth hooked in an overhead kick from the wing and I sneaked in at the back post to knock it home. The second wasn't far different, with a hard and low cross fired in by Eoin Jess for me to tuck away. When you have service from both wings like that, it's sometimes harder not to score.

They were both close-range goals and from that day on I was firmly established as the penalty-box predator the supporters had craved for so long. Actually that wasn't what my game had always been about – if you watch back my goals from Swindon or Huddersfield, you see them crashing in from all angles and distances. It was as I got older and, perhaps, wiser that I became a penalty-box player. I ended up with the same rewards but with a far smaller part of the pitch to cover. As I got older, that was a blessing.

I'm fortunate that I am able to watch back almost every goal I've ever scored. From the beginning of my career I made a point of taping television coverage, whether on the local Monday night news or on highlights programmes, of the goals I scored. When I was at Pittodrie, Lesley Campbell in the marketing department helped me transfer everything from old tapes to DVDs after she had moved to join AVC Media. AVC had helped countless clubs, as well as the national team, with footage and it was a big help for them to do the work for me. It means I've got a nice collection to look back on and keep the memories alive, including my first goals for Aberdeen.

Pretty much as soon as I'd scored those two goals against Hibs, the comparisons began. Even Alex McLeish had me down as the next Joe Harper. I never wanted to be that, I far preferred to be the first Duncan Shearer than try to emulate anyone else's achievements.

Willie Miller took me to one side after the Hibs game and told me it was a good start – I said it was a good start for both of us. Willie was starting out as a manager in his own right. It was his first full season and it was his team being judged now.

Not long after the second of my two against Hibs I was taken off, replaced by Eoin Jess. To say I wasn't happy was an understatement – I was on a hat-trick, on my debut. It could have been the perfect start.

It was David Wylie, the physio, who took me aside and explained the thinking behind it. Apparently, Willie felt two goals would be enough, that any more would have raised the expectation levels to fever pitch. In the cold light of day I could understand the logic. The Dons fans had watched their share of prolific scorers over the years and the prospect of having a new man to pin their hopes on was bound to cause a bit of a stir. With Celtic in the next match it was a case of keeping things calm and trying to avoid too much hype.

After the win against Hibs, I scored in the 1–1 midweek draw against Celtic at Pittodrie and we went on to beat Falkirk at

Brockville a few days later to put ourselves in pole position. We were full of confidence when we went through to Ibrox for the first match against Rangers that season. The 3–1 defeat we suffered wasn't in the script and from that point on we were playing catch-up.

We only lost seven of the forty-four Premier Division games that season, but the key was that three of those were against Rangers. When I scored the only goal of the game in the penultimate match of the season to beat Walter Smith's side at Pittodrie, in the fourth and final league match against them, it at least got the monkey off our back. As far as the title was concerned it was too little to late. We had to settle for second place, finishing nine points off the pace when it was still two points for a win.

It was the same in the cup competitions. We just couldn't get over the final hurdle when Rangers stood in the way. In the League Cup, or the Skol Cup as it was at that time, we went in at the second-round stage and breezed past Arbroath with a 4–0 win at Gayfield. A couple of goals from Mixu and one apiece from myself and Eoin set us up for a home tie against Dunfermline, when Mixu was on target again to take us through 1–0. In the quarter-finals we were drawn to play Falkirk at Brockville and it was a perfect time to get my first hat-trick for the club, with big Brian Irvine also hitting the net in a 4–1 win.

I got my first taste of Hampden when we faced Celtic in the semi-final, with Rangers up against St Johnstone twenty-four hours earlier and cantering to a 3–1 win. We knew if we could get through our tie it was Rangers waiting for us in the final and given the strength of the rivalry between the clubs it was a huge incentive for us. A cup final against Rangers was what the supporters wanted and it was certainly what the players hoped for too.

It was a cagey semi against Celtic but when Eoin Jess scored in the first half it settled our nerves and we shut out the rest of the game to earn a place in the final. It was late October when we ran out at Hampden again to take on Rangers. Going into the game we'd had two 3–1 wins in the league, the first against Hibs and then another against Falkirk. Rangers had hammered St Johnstone 5–1 and then edged past Hibs 1–0 to stay top, so we were two form sides.

As you'd expect, there was nothing between us. Stuart McCall had put Rangers ahead in the first half but I grabbed an equaliser, a sweetly struck right-foot volley, to take the game into extra time. Then disaster struck. Gary Smith put past Theo Snelders and it was curtains for us. That own goal made it 2–1 and that was how it finished. It was a crushing disappointment and a real blow to watch them pick up the first trophy of the season. It was a horrible experience for Gary, who had been in smashing form for us and was still just a young man. On the other hand, it was at that point that it began to hit me that I wasn't getting any younger and that there may not be too many cup finals left for me to try and pick up a winner's medal. I'd been involved in promotions with Swindon and Blackburn and I'd made it into the PFA team of the year in England, but I still did not have a medal to call my own.

What I did have as I trudged off the pitch at Hampden was an envelope in my hand. I'd been handed it by a man I'd never met before and never saw again. I was only told, 'This will make up for the disappointment.' I never gave it a second thought and stuffed it my pocket when I got back to the dressing room. It wasn't until we were on the bus going back up the road that I found it again and opened it up to find I'd won a prize as the last scorer in the competition, with Gary's own goal obviously not counting. The reward was a stay at the Gleneagles Hotel. Michele was expecting our son William at that stage, and we booked our place when bad weather gave us an unexpected weekend off. We checked in and were told that the package included an £82 drinks tab. Michele obviously wasn't drinking anything stronger than orange juice at that point, and I thought I was in for a little party until I saw the wine list, with the cheapest bottle coming in at £60. Then the £82 made a bit more sense and I ordered myself a nice red. It was a fantastic gesture and we had a wonderful time, staying in a beautiful suite, but I would have swapped it for a winner's medal.

As galling as it was to lose in the final, it at least showed we were on the right track and by the time the Scottish Cup got up and running for us in January 1993 the League Cup final was a fading memory. We came into the Scottish Cup at the third-round stage, beating Hamilton 4–1 at Pittodrie in a game I sat out. I was back in time for the next game, a 2–0 win against Dundee United, with Eoin Jess scoring both, and got my first ever Scottish Cup goal from the penalty spot when we drew 1–1 with Clydebank in the quarter-final at Pittodrie. They proved to be tough customers that season and gave us a fright in the replay, before we came through to win 4–3 and tee up a semi-final against Hibs at Tynecastle. Hearts were head-to-head with Rangers at Parkhead on the same day and both ties were close-run affairs.

While Rangers were beating Hearts 2–1 in Glasgow, I was watching from the stand as we sneaked through 1–0 against Hibs, thanks to Scott Booth's goal in the second half.

The Scottish Cup was brilliant to be involved in. The last time I had played a tie in the competition was as a Clach player and the aims were a little bit different then from the ones we had now with Aberdeen. Having gone all the way to the final in the League Cup, we went into the Scottish Cup believing we could win it.

There was a two-week gap between the end of the league season and the cup final, which was staged at Celtic Park because of the redevelopment work at Hampden that year. It gave us a leisurely build-up and we were taken away on the eve of the final to be tucked away in a hotel in preparation for the game.

I roomed with Paul Kane and we had become good friends during the season. He had come into his own after Eoin Jess had suffered a broken leg in the cup tie against Clydebank, slotting into the midfield and doing a cracking job in there. We were up in the room when Paul took a call from his dad, trying to sound out the team for the following day. Paul was excited – he was sure he'd be in the team. He'd been in the Hibs side that was battered by Aberdeen in the League Cup final in 1985 so this was his big chance to make amends.

I was too, given he had played in every game leading up to the final. It was touch and go whether Eoin Jess would be back in time to play against Rangers. Paul had come into the team in his place and done a great job, so the smart money was on him keeping his place and Eoin making the bench at best. In the week leading up to the game, Eoin had trained away without a problem but it was going to be a big risk for him to come back without any match practice and play in a cup final against Rangers.

We gathered in the morning and had our pre-match meal and then sat down for Willie to go through the team. He ran through from one to eleven, with no mention of Paul Kane. Paul's head went down, and then when the subs had been listed, and again no mention, his head dipped even further. In all my years in football, it was the cruellest thing I have ever seen. There was no tactical reason for what had happened, particularly given the versatility Paul could offer. He should have started and at the very least would have been very useful to have on the bench. But he wasn't, he was bombed out completely without a word of explanation.

As it happened the gamble didn't pay off. Eoin played but really struggled to get going on what was an absolutely scorching day. It sapped the energy out of all of us, but for someone who had been out injured long-term it must have been an even bigger struggle. To be fair to Eoin, we all toiled and Rangers ran out pretty comfortable winners.

They were strong and ran out with Andy Goram in goal, a back four of Neil Murray, David Robertson, Richard Gough and Dave McPherson and a midfield of Pieter Huistra, John Brown, Stuart McCall and Ian Ferguson, with Mark Hateley and Ian Durrant adding a bit of bite up front.

There was no inferiority though, I would argue that on paper we had a better side. Theo Snelders, Stewart McKimmie, Stephen Wright, Alex McLeish and Brian Irvine were a solid unit in defence. We had Lee Richardson and Brian Grant in the middle of the park and pace and power going forward in the shape of Paul Mason, Scott Booth, Mixu Paatelainen and myself.

When Neil Murray and Mark Hateley put Rangers 2–0 before half-time, we faced an uphill struggle. Lee Richardson pulled one back after the break but we just couldn't find the equaliser we needed to force extra time.

After the game we were taken back to St Andrews for what could have been post-match celebrations but turned into a bit of a wake. I went away and got changed out of the club gear and came back downstairs in the hotel, where everyone was sitting around moping. Everyone apart from Paul, who had gone missing. I eventually tracked him down and he was swearing and cursing the decision not to let him play. I managed to persuade him to get a taxi back to Edinburgh and get as far away from the manager as he could, before he said anything he might regret.

It was Willie's job to pick the team. He was paid to make those difficult decisions. Only he knows why he chose to approach it the way he did. Willie had pressures of his own to contend with. He'd been given a fair amount of money to spend and had the nucleus of a good side at Pittodrie. The problem was that good was never going to be enough, it had to be the best to meet the ambitions of the manager and the board.

To end the season empty-handed, after coming so close in every competition, left a big cloud hanging over us. In the current climate, you have to think that finishing second would be considered a major achievement – but for us, it just wasn't good enough. Nobody took it harder than Willie Miller and he went back to the drawing board that summer, searching for the magic formula to cut down Rangers in their prime.

On a personal level it had been a very good year, on and off the park. I finished leading scorer at Pittodrie with twenty-eight goals, eight ahead of Mixu, and the supporters had taken me to their hearts. Along the way I had broken Frank McDougall's club record of twenty-two Premier Division goals in a single season, helped in no small part by back-to-back league hat-tricks in a 7–0 trouncing of Partick Thistle and a 6–2 canter against Hearts. With another hat-trick against Falkirk in the League Cup – when we won 4–1 at Brockville in the quarter-finals – it turned out to be a very productive first season for me.

At home, my son was born in May 1993. The baby was due in the build-up to the Scottish Cup final and the manager kept telling me that 2 May would be a good date. I guessed that date would have fitted in well with the preparations and sure enough young William Shearer made his entrance on 2 May. It turned out it was the same date as Willie Miller's birthday and when he found out the new arrival shared his name I think he thought I was looking for brownie points. He told me I'd definitely be playing in the team on the back of it. As it happens, we chose the name after the baby's Uncle Willie and the similarities between the two of them are uncanny at times. My boy has the same athletic build and the same amazing long fingers that my brother had. I knew he would never have children of his own because of the accident and wanted him to feel part of my William's young life.

A Scottish Cup winner's medal a few weeks later would have put the icing on the cake but I went away at the end of it hoping that the next season would bring even bigger and better things for Aberdeen. I did not realise I would have another couple of years to wait for a trophy.

13

PRIDE OF SCOTLAND

'Shearer for Scotland.' That was the phrase Willie Miller greeted me with when I picked up the phone at the house. I just said to him: 'That would be nice.' As far as I was concerned the chance had passed me by, so when Willie said, 'You're in the squad', my heart skipped a beat. It was a dream come true and at the age of thirty it meant all the more to me.

The call came in February 1993, just a few months before the end of my first season with Aberdeen. I was invited to join the squad for a World Cup qualifier against Malta at Ibrox by Andy Roxburgh and I hadn't the slightest idea I was in the frame. Although I was always confident of my ability to score goals, I felt age was against me and put any thoughts of Scotland out of my mind.

When I went to Aberdeen I became good friends with Graham Herd, the owner of the Dolphin chip shop on Chapel Street. The business provided me with a sponsored car and you could often find me through the back of the shop – and not just because I liked the produce. Graham was adamant that if I kept scoring goals for Aberdeen I'd get the call for Scotland. I told him there was no chance.

When it did happen for me it was totally out of the blue. Willie's call was the first I knew about it, with the club getting notified before the player. You don't get a call from the SFA or the coach; the club is responsible for telling you and then a letter arrives with the travel details and rest of the information.

The benefit for me was that I was far from alone. At that time Aberdeen had a squad peppered with internationals. That season we had Alex McLeish, Stewart McKimmie, Brian Irvine, Stephen Wright, Scott Booth, Eoin Jess and myself involved in the Scotland side. It was an extraordinary period for the club and I don't think even the glory days of the 1980s brought the same level of involvement at Pittodrie.

Being in that sort of company at club level had obviously brought me into view, which was strange for me since I was doing exactly the same as I had been doing for virtually my whole career.

Being back up the road was the key to getting into the Scotland side. It's ironic when you consider the situation now, where playing in England, even at Championship level, is considered far more desirable than in the SPL when it comes to enhancing international credentials.

I didn't regret the decision to stay in England for as long as I had, even if it did harm my Scotland chances. I enjoyed every minute with Chelsea, Huddersfield, Swindon and Blackburn. I came back over the border when it felt like it was the right time and fortunately that gave me the opportunity to play for my country.

It was bizarre going into that environment at the age I was. As a thirty-year-old I was one of the most senior players, but I was there as a total novice in international football. Unlike most, playing for the A-team was my first experience of playing for Scotland at any level. I hadn't had the benefit of trying it out at youth level, under-twenty or even as part of a B-squad.

I was nervous, excited and curious all at the same time, as well as being ripe for a wind-up. When I joined the squad at the team hotel near Greenock, I was paired with Ian Ferguson of

Rangers as my room-mate, but it turned out it wasn't Ian I had to watch out for. After getting settled in I went for a wee walk along by the river in the hotel grounds and met Maurice Malpas along the way. We were due for a team meeting at 6pm and I asked Mo where we had to gather. He told me that because it was such a nice night we were having it outside, not far from where the two of us were speaking. I knew Andy Roxburgh was very regimented in his approach and a stickler for discipline, which suited me fine. I'd been brought up to always be on time, so that evening I wandered down to the river with ten minutes to spare and was the first one there. The clocked ticked round to 5.55pm and there was still no sign of the rest of the squad. Six o'clock came and went, with still no sign. I gave it another five minutes or so before I went back in to ask at reception what the hold-up was, only to be told that the meeting was along the corridor in the library. I walked in sheepishly, with Andy shooting daggers at me as I interrupted his meeting. Maurice was there too, staring at the ground and no doubt doing his best to stop himself from cracking up. He'd stitched me up a beauty.

I was on the bench that day and didn't get on, with Ally McCoist and Eoin Jess getting the nod and John Robertson making an appearance as a substitute. We won comfortably, with Ally scoring either side of half-time and Pat Nevin getting the third and final goal of the game towards the end.

In the dressing room afterwards, they started handing out the caps. They missed me out and it wasn't until the rest of the subs who hadn't played had been bypassed that it dawned on me – I still wasn't getting the cap I'd been dreaming of.

You tend to get greedy when it comes to Scotland. At one point I would have been happy just to have been involved. When I found myself in the squad I wanted that first appearance and first cap, then I wanted to start a game and get a goal. Then when you've got one cap and one goal you want more and so it goes on. Pulling on that dark blue jersey was such a buzz for me, especially as a long-standing member of the Tartan Army.

I first travelled to Hampden as a teenager, and from that moment on I was hooked, travelling the world watching Scotland. The most elaborate trip was in 1986 when myself and three friends from Fort William jetted off to Mexico for the World Cup finals. 'Go Go' Blackmore, Alan McKinnon and Davie Neil made up the crew and we headed off in optimistic mood, with the three of them booking five weeks off work just in case Scotland made the final. I had all the time in the world as it obviously fell during the close season and we decided we'd stay out for the duration come what may.

David Speedie, my Chelsea buddy, had agreed to help us out with tickets and everything was set up. Then disaster struck – David was bombed out of the squad at the last minute by Alex Ferguson. It was a late, late decision and David was absolutely devastated. He'd even received his blazer and kit for the trip before Fergie had a change of heart and replaced him. I gather Speedie gave Alex both barrels when he found out. I felt so sorry for David and genuinely believe he would have been a tremendous asset in that squad and in that climate with all of his energy and commitment. Speedie may have been small in stature but he was a defender's nightmare, quick and aggressive as well as being able to jump higher than anyone I've ever seen. The spring he had made him such a deceptive player and an aerial threat despite his lack of height.

While David was left at home, the intrepid quartet from Lochaber headed out undaunted. We had an absolutely marvellous time in Mexico and loved every minute. We cheered on Scotland every step of the way and when our team went out we hung around to soak up the atmosphere as the final loomed. We were outside the stadium on the day of the final, where tickets were changing hands for frightening amounts of money, before unfolding our map and picking a spot to round off the trip. Acapulco sounded good and that's where we ended up.

Whenever my own football commitments would allow I always found time to watch Scotland and I've been to the World Cup a couple of times now, with France 98 my second taste of the big occasion. I was there in Paris for the opening game against Brazil, although it's a bit of a blur. I'd travelled with five mates from Aberdeen and on the way to the ground we were stopped every ten yards by groups of Dons supporters who wanted to share a beer and I ended up half-cut by the time I took my seat.

By then my days as an international player were well behind me but I was fortunate to at least have sampled football at that level and lived the dream of turning out for Scotland.

I had a year to wait to get my run-out after that first call up from Andy Roxburgh. After the Malta game early in 1993, I was back in the squad the following month for the 0–0 draw against Germany, again at Ibrox, but again I didn't get any game time. It was when Craig Brown took over from Andy at the end of that campaign that I eventually got my big break, making my debut in April 1994 in a friendly against Austria in Vienna.

Craig was a different operator from Andy, who was a very intense man indeed. When Andy was focused, there was absolutely nothing that could knock him off his stride and everything was ordered, from tactics and training to team talks and the game plan itself. Craig, having worked closely with Andy for so long, had many of the same traits but he was a different character and a lot closer to the players. Craig knew when to have a laugh and when to be serious, with a great sense of humour and bit of a sense of mischief about him too. When Craig took over he had Alex Miller as his assistant and Alex was the polar opposite, serious to the point of being dour. You can't argue with what Alex Miller has achieved in coaching but I think I'd rather go through life with a smile on my face.

I think Craig appreciated my personality and to be honest I also reckon he had a bit of a soft spot for Highlanders. He was such a patriotic character and I think he felt the likes of myself and John McGinlay epitomised the Scottish spirit. John was a big pal of mine, having grown up in Caol with me. When I came on from the bench against Austria for my first cap it was John I replaced and it couldn't have been scripted any better, standing there shaking his hand as I prepared for one of the proudest moments of my career.

I was given fifteen minutes against the Austrians to get a taste for the international game and it passed in a flash. The abiding memory is of their big striker, Toni Polster, coming off second best after a bit of jostling with Brian Irvine in the box, before turning and dredging up something from the depths of his throat that he spat straight in big Brian's face. Not surprisingly Brian went ballistic, chasing the Austrian and giving him a real blast. It transpired that he'd gone after him to say: 'Don't you ever, ever do that again.' It was typical of Brian – rather than effing and blinding he chose to give the guy a stern telling off. Polster, who must have thought Brian was about to lay one on him, was left relieved and probably a bit bemused by it all.

When you look at the team for that game in Vienna, you realise how good a state the international team was in during that era. Jim Leighton was in goals, with all of his experience and composure – there was an embarrassment of riches in that department for the manager, when you consider Andy Goram was also on the go. The defence also had a very settled look to it, with Stewart McKimmie and Tom Boyd on the flanks and Colin Hendry, Brian Irvine and Alan McLaren through the middle. Alan's versatility was a big plus and he was often pushed slightly further forward into a man-marking role, anchoring the midfield.

John Collins, Gary McAllister and Billy McKinlay were all class acts in midfield and that day it was John McGinlay and Eoin Jess in attack. As well as me, the subs used were Ian Ferguson, Stuart McCall and Pat Nevin. In short, Craig Brown wasn't short of options right the way through the team and had a lot of experienced and very reliable campaigners to call on.

We played Austria in April 1994 as a warm-up to the qualifying campaign for Euro 96 and rounded off the preparations by playing the Netherlands the following month in Utrecht. After the disappointment of missing out on a place at the World Cup in America, there was a determination not to let the same happen for the European Championships – especially since they would be held across the border. To have had to sit back and watch England host the tournament with no Scottish involvement would have been absolutely horrific and there was a lot of talk among the squad about how much it meant for us to make sure we were there.

The game against Holland was a good test before the competitive games began and a chance for Craig to begin putting his mark on the team, having stepped out of the shadow of Andy Roxburgh.

As in the game against Austria, I was introduced as a late substitute. It was a memorable match to be involved in and marked Ruud Gullit's swansong as an international footballer. To be lining up alongside Gullit and the rest of the Dutch superstars was inspiring. I'd been around the block as a club professional by then but I was still awestruck in the company of players of Gullit's stature.

All of that ends when the whistle sounds to start the game, but we were given a bit of a lesson that day. Brian Irvine in particular was pulled all over the place – and it was no surprise, given his preparation for the match. The game was played in the last week in May, well after our season with Aberdeen had finished. The Dons players in the Scotland squad had been given the option of taking time off between the last league game and the Netherlands fixture or travelling with the rest of the Pittodrie players for a post-season trip to Canada.

All apart from Brian decided to stay at home. He went away to Canada for four or five days and then came back just in time for the international friendly. We trained at Broadwood before flying out to Holland and Brian fell fast asleep on the journey from Cumbernauld to the team hotel in East Kilbride. The next morning he looked awful, still exhausted, and he fell asleep on the bus to the airport and then again on the flight. Playing against the Dutch when you're full of beans is bad enough but to take them on when you're shattered is ten times worse.

By the time I got the nod from Craig to go on in the seventy-sixth minute, again replacing John McGinlay, we were 3–0 down and toiling. The bright spot for me was that I salvaged a bit of pride for the team and broke my duck with Scotland when I got my head to a lovely curling Eoin Jess cross to the back post and tucked it away. I got my cap against Austria and my goal against the Netherlands, so the boxes were being ticked off one by one. All I needed to complete the set was to start a game and I didn't have too long to wait.

14

THE ROAD TO WEMBLEY

The World Cup without Scotland in 1994 was painful to watch. For as long as I could remember we had been involved in the finals and all of a sudden we had lost that place among the big boys. It hurt the fans and it hurt the players, so while everyone else on the planet was sitting down to watch the action from the USA there was a totally different focus among the Scotland camp.

By the time the games in America kicked off, we were already looking towards Euro 96 with a burning desire to make sure we were represented. Although we had missed out on the World Cup, our stock in the international game was still relatively high and that ensured the qualifying draw was reasonable.

Russia and Greece were the two main threats as far as we were concerned. Both had been involved in the finals in America but had hardly set the heather alight, with the Russians winning just one of their group games and the Greeks losing all three. Finland were the other team in our pool, Group 8, that we had to be wary of, while San Marino and the Faroe Islands were always expected to be battling to avoid the wooden spoon.

Only top spot in the group would guarantee qualification, with the six best runners-up also going through to the finals in England at the end of the campaign. With pride dented from our absence from the World Cup, getting off to a positive start was vital if we were to build confidence and bring back the belief that we belonged at the top table.

The fixtures sent us away to Finland in the opening match of the qualifiers, in September 1994, just a week after I'd scored a hat-trick against Partick Thistle in a League Cup tie at Firhill. I guess that didn't do my chances of getting a game any harm and, sure enough, when Craig named the team for the match against the Finns I was in the starting line-up.

I had turned thirty-two less than a fortnight before the game and to finally get my chance to play a full ninety minutes for Scotland was the best present anyone could have given me. To be handed the famous dark blue No. 9 shirt was the icing on the cake.

Andy Walker was the man Craig chose to partner me in a game we knew was going to be a battle. The opposition had my old Pittodrie mate Mixu Paatelainen in their side and, like Mixu, they were a strong and physical side who knew how to play the game. It may be that there used to be some easy games in international football but by then the tide was turning and every match carried potential pitfalls.

We had Andy Goram between the sticks, with a back four of Stewart McKimmie, Tom Boyd, Craig Levein and Colin Hendry. It was a rock-solid foundation and with Alan McLaren man-marking the Ajax star Jari Litmanen to perfection, there was no way through for the home side. In midfield John Collins, Gary McAllister and Paul McStay were pulling the strings in behind Andy Walker and me.

A point wouldn't have been a disgrace in a difficult away tie, but we came away from Finland with a win that gave us the perfect start on the long road to Euro 96. We beat them 2–0 and I justified my inclusion with the opener, a goal that Craig Brown has described as one of the best, if not the best, Scotland have ever scored. That wasn't a tribute to my finish but to the whole

Captain fantastic: That's me in the centre with the cup after skippering the Caol School shinty team to our first success in the sport for many years.

On my way: Me in my younger days as a promising player with Clach.

Spot the difference: Another Shearer in full flow on the football field, this time my big brother David pictured during his days with Clach in the 1970s as he set off on the path that made him a star with Middlesbrough.

Bright lights of London: Me in action for the Chelsea reserves soon after moving to Stamford Bridge from the Highland League.

On the up: Paul Davis and David O'Leary of Arsenal close in on me during a cup tie in my Huddersfield days.

UNISYS
COMPUTER

WEMBLEY STADIUM
SUNDERLAND 0
SWINDON TOWN 1

The biggest stage of all: The scoreboard tells the story in the play-off final victory against Sunderland at a packed Wembley Stadium.

Let the good times roll: Relief, joy and pride as the Swindon team celebrated our play-off success at Wembley.

A day at the races: Glenn Hoddle and I at the Cheltenham races during my Swindon days. I loved working with Glenn and he improved me as a player.

On the Blackburn beat: My short time at Ewood Park came during an exciting time for the club as we won promotion to the top flight.

The start of something special: Willie Miller welcomes Michele and I to Pittodrie following my transfer from Blackburn.

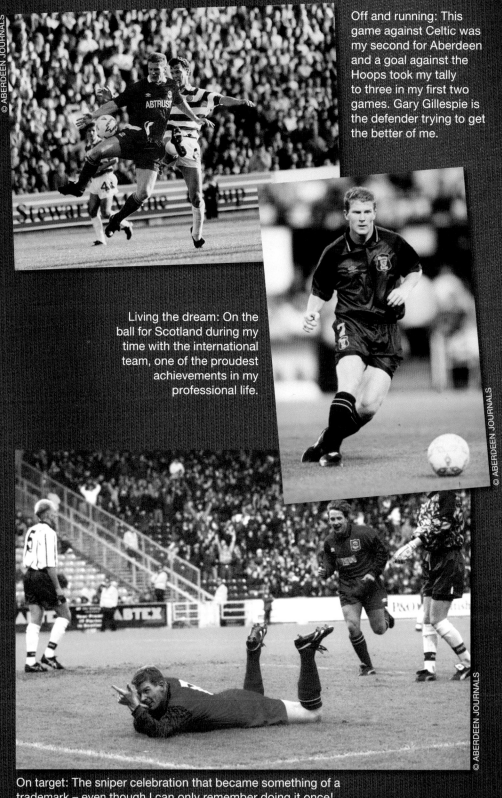

Off and running: This game against Celtic was my second for Aberdeen and a goal against the Hoops took my tally to three in my first two games. Gary Gillespie is the defender trying to get the better of me.

Living the dream: On the ball for Scotland during my time with the international team, one of the proudest achievements in my professional life.

On target: The sniper celebration that became something of a trademark – even though I can only remember doing it once!

The party begins: Billy
Dodds and Stewart
McKimmie join in the League
Cup celebrations in 1995.

Hands on the prize
at last: The League
Cup is heading back
to Aberdeen after our
win against Dundee at
Hampden in 1995.

Back where it all began: Having started my playing career in Inverness with Clach,
I wound down my days on the frontline back in the city with Caley Thistle.

The homecoming: When Steve Paterson and I checked in at
Pittodrie in 2002 it was a dream opportunity for both of us.

Getting down to business: I've worked hard to complete my coaching badges
and enjoy every minute on the training pitch. This picture, with David Zdrilic and
Markus Heikkinen, was during our second season at Pittodrie.

Tower of strength: My brother William, pictured here with me a couple of years before his death, had to show enormous courage during his life.

Mother's pride: My mum died before I made my way in the world but I know she would have been proud of my career and my family.

The happy couple: Michele and I on our wedding day – with my dad's house in the background!

The boys are back in town: John McGinlay and I proudly show off the scrolls we received when we were awarded the freedom of Caol. Pictured along with John, Michele and I (front row) are my sisters Catherine (back row, far right) and Alison next to my brother Finlay as well as my brother David (back row, third from left) and close friends from the town.

Then: Hayley and William try on Dad's Scotland caps and shirts for size.

And now: William and Hayley as they are now, a young man and lady who have made Michele and I so proud.

Guiding light: My mother-in-law Nita, pictured here with my son William and me, was my landlady when I first arrived in London to play for Chelsea.

Success at last: Ghillie Steve Shand and me with the first salmon I ever landed, caught during one of my annual outings with Nicky Walker at Balindalloch Castle on the River Spey. Within minutes I'd hooked my second one after years of trying.

A time to celebrate: My father (left) and father-in-law Michael with Hayley as the family celebrated her Holy Communion.

build-up. There must have been twenty-six passes leading up to Tom Boyd's cross from the left and I popped up to flash home the header that settled any nerves. John Collins made it 2–0 in the second half to get the campaign off to a flying start.

The Tartan Army were in good voice and as we trooped off the park it was Pat Nevin who drew my attention to one man in the crowd desperately trying to catch my eye. It turned out to be a supporter by the name of Hughie, who had made it over to the Olympic Stadium for the game. After wishing me well, he threw a Clach lapel badge onto the track for me as a keepsake of the day I got my first start and second goal for Scotland. I'm guessing the last time he saw me score a goal in the flesh would have been back at Grant Street Park in the early 1980s.

I tried to get Mixu's shirt as another memento of the game but it turned out it wasn't just the SFA who had a reputation for being thrifty with the pennies. A slightly embarrassed Mixu had to tell me they weren't allowed to swap jerseys. It was no hardship because I ended up keeping all of my Scotland tops for my own collection. They're among the most precious possessions from my career, although I did have to make sacrifices to get them.

My goal against the Finns came at a fairly substantial personal price. As I got my head to Tom's cross, a Finnish defender got his head to mine and knocked me out for the briefest of moments. In that time I did enough damage to wreck my season. When I blacked out, my knees buckled as my full dead weight came down on them, damaging the medial ligament in each of them. To do one would have been bad but to do both was freakish. Having watched it back, I've seen exactly what happened. I looked like a giraffe who'd had a good drink with the way my legs collapsed and knees knocked together.

The problem was that I didn't know at the time the damage I'd done and I played on, fuelled by pure adrenalin, for the full ninety minutes. It was a nightmare to dance at Victoria's night-club in Glasgow when we got back on home soil – and that was when I knew I was in trouble. Sure enough, a thorough check-up back at Pittodrie diagnosed the problem and I was out of action for eight weeks initially and then another six after an abortive attempt to come back too soon.

I kept the Victoria's part of the story to myself, especially when Willie Miller started asking questions about what treat-ment I'd had after the game. Having been there, done that and worn the T-shirt with Scotland I reckon he could probably have guessed I hadn't been wrapped up in ice packs in my hotel room. It wasn't until the following morning that the knees became really, really painful and by then the damage had been done. It was going to be a long way back, both for club and country.

In the months that I was back at Pittodrie battling back to fitness, Craig and the team were ploughing on in the qualifiers. I missed the 5–1 win against the Faroe Islands at Hampden and a 1–1 draw against Russia at the national stadium, as well as the 1–0 defeat in Greece. That match in Athens was a serious blow to our hopes of winning the group, or even finishing second, with both the Russians and the Greeks getting off to a brilliant start and hammering in the goals as they won every one of their matches.

It was March 1995 when I finally made it back into Scotland colours, called up for the return match against the Russians at the Luzhniki Stadium in Moscow. It was a make-or-break match for us and we knew that if we lost it could kill our qualification hopes stone dead.

That trip to Moscow was an incredible experience, not least because of the Baltic weather conditions. An eastern European winter is not for the faint-hearted and when we ran out at the ground for a training session on the eve of the match we found ourselves in the middle of a snow storm. It was always going to be a light session. Craig was never willing to run through anything involving shape or tactics on the opposition park, for the obvious reason that the other team's coaching staff would be watching. All of the detailed work in terms of tactics and set pieces was done on flip charts in the privacy of our hotel, as far from prying eyes as was possible.

Undaunted by the blizzards, Craig was determined to carry on with some filming he wanted to do. The idea was to get some footage of a rotation drill that he wanted to show the various youth teams in the Scotland set-up. The hitch was that every time the ball landed at John Spencer's feet he fired off a shot instead of passing it. Craig stopped everyone in their tracks and explained it again, telling John: 'It's quite simple: we just want you to pass the ball round in sequence.' We ran through the drill again and then the ball fell to wee John – who rattled off another shot at goal. Craig was getting more and more exasperated and hauled us all off the park. As we trudged off, John turned to Craig and said: 'Those youth teams learned nothing from that.' He may as well have winked as he said it, but he got us off the hook that night and back into the warmth of the changing rooms. If it had been anyone else I'm pretty sure Craig would have gone ballistic but Spencer was cheeky enough to get away with it.

When the game rolled around, it wasn't just the weather we had to contend with. The Russians were a very handy team and it was the first and only time I've ever felt scared on a football park. I was on the bench and came on for Darren Jackson with around quarter of an hour to go, with the team still hanging on for a point in a game locked at 0–0. The pace was frantic and the boys had done so well to battle away right through to the closing stages, working towards what would be a very respectable point. One of the first things I had to do when I came on was to help defend a corner and when the ball broke out wide I found myself in one of the most terrifying places I'd ever been

– one-on-one with Andrei Kanchelskis. I'd only ever seen Andrei on television with Manchester United, but I knew enough from that to realise that if he pushed the ball past me I'd be left trailing in his wake. In my mind I was ready to take a booking or worse, do whatever I had to, as long as he didn't get past me. As it happened I managed to close him down and force him to play the ball back, away from the danger area and I could breathe again. We played out the rest of the ninety minutes, got the point and got back home with mission accomplished.

That game also marked my old Swindon skipper Colin Calderwood's debut for the international team, a well deserved honour for a superb defender. Colin went on to win thirty-six caps, despite not starting at that level until he was thirty, an incredible tally in such a short space of time. Colin and I went through a lot together at Swindon and we became very good friends, a friendship that has stood the test of time. We're still close to this day and I have an awful lot of respect for him as a player, as a coach and as a person. When Colin ran out against Brazil in the opening game of the World Cup at France 98, it was a fitting highlight for a great Scotland servant.

The journey for him had begun in Russia in 1995, just as my own international career was drawing to a close. The match in Moscow was my fourth cap and it turned out I had just another five months left with Craig's squad. It was long enough to help the team towards a place at Euro 96, with our point in Moscow and then Russia's 3–0 thumping of Greece, helping our cause no end. Those results opened the whole group up again and all we had to do was to make sure we kept on picking up points.

My fifth appearance was against San Marino in Serravalle in April 1995, where a small crowd gathered for what was a big occasion for myself and John McGinlay. That day the two of us played up front together for Scotland to give our little village of Caol something to shout about. There were less than 3,000 people in the ground for the game but back home in Fort William there were a lot more than that cheering us on. In the build-up to the game the television crews had motored up to the west coast as soon as news broke that the pair of us would be playing together and it was a really memorable time for John and me.

We won the game 2–0, with goals from John Collins and Colin Calderwood, but the real celebrations were when we got back to Fort William. We were invited along to a reception hosted by the council to mark the international double act. The event also celebrated Fort William's victory in the Camanachd Cup. John and I were each allowed to invite a dozen guests and, with a free bar open all night, it turned into a really great bash. I think we ended up running the bar dry, but nobody complained. After all, it's not every day that Caol has two players in the Scotland team.

Our reward was to be awarded the freedom of Caol during the celebration, a tremendous honour for two humble lads from the village. Aside from the honour of the title, it enables John and I to drive our sheep through the area. It isn't something I've put to use yet, but who knows what the future might hold! In all seriousness, it was a great feeling to be back home and to know that we had done everyone proud with our efforts for Scotland.

Craig stuck with the same partnership when we went to Toftir to play the Faroes in June that year and it worked. We won 2–0, with Billy McKinlay scoring the first and John grabbing the second, to keep the qualifying campaign on track.

Toftir was the weirdest place I've ever been to. Even getting there was like no other journey. After flying into the Faroes we had to get a ferry for the second leg of the journey, with the boat going upstream in a fast-flowing river before turning, in a well-timed manoeuvre, and drifting back down the way to a slipway on the opposite bank from where we'd started. The captain had to time it to perfection to avoid the boat being pulled down by the current.

After that we had an hour on a bus to the team hotel, where I was rooming with my old mate McGinlay. That was an education in itself. John went back to his room for a kip in the afternoon but came back minutes later, moaning he couldn't get to sleep because somebody was mowing the roof of our room. Only in the Faroes. All the chalet-type buildings had grass roofs as it happened, and that wasn't the only unusual way of life out there.

All of the players were gathered downstairs on the day before the game when one of the Tartan Army came in carrying a big bag. He laid it out on the table, called Colin Hendry across and proudly handed it over. Colin opened it up to find a sheep's head inside. Apparently it's a good-luck gesture in the Faroes. Colin just about jumped out of his skin when he saw it. That was one souvenir he wasn't going to be taking home with him.

The stadium in Toftir, set into a cliff, is as quirky as the customs. Fortunately we weren't distracted by the surroundings and gained maximum points to send us away happy.

There was a two-month break before we faced up to Greece at Hampden. After six away matches with Scotland, it was my big chance to play in front of a home crowd. When Craig told me I was in the side it was a tremendous buzz. I played alongside Darren Jackson and we both got the usual instruction: 'Give us a good shift.' That was always Craig's mantra. He wanted you to knock your pan in for an hour or so before he sent on the fresh legs. He had options to be able to do that too, with Ally McCoist and John Robertson both on the bench and champing at the bit to get on.

I did what was asked of me, chasing and harrying for a good seventy minutes, before eventually getting the signal to come off. I shook Ally's hand on the way off and made my way to the dugout, bending down to undo my tie-ups. Just as I bent down there was a huge roar right the way round Hampden and I turned round to see Super Ally running away from goal with his arms outstretched in that familiar pose. Old Golden Balls had struck again. I'd run myself into the ground and he went on to take the glory!

It transpired that the shift against the Greeks in that 1–0 win was my last duty in dark blue. I was involved in the squad for the Finland game the following month but was carrying an injury and had to concede defeat just before we went out for a training session once the squad had gathered on the west coast. Andy Goram, Ally McCoist and John Robertson were all struggling too.

Ally made it onto the bench in the end, but for John, Andy and me there was no chance. Craig Brown gave us the choice of either going home or staying with the squad. I didn't need to be asked twice. I wanted to stay and lend a bit of moral support if nothing else.

Andy and John were the same and when we went out for a team meal that night we were allowed to have more than the normal glass of wine with dinner. I was never a great wine drinker, other than the occasional glass, but that night I had a crash course in the stuff.

The three of us wounded soldiers ended up going back to Andy's room and got through a good few bottles, talking football into the small hours. I was rooming with Colin Calderwood for that gathering and in the early hours of the morning I thought it was time to get back to the room.

The bedrooms were all named after golfers. Its bad enough trying to find a room with a number when you've had a few drinks but when you're trying to remember if you're looking for the Tom Weiskopf or some other name from the great and good it's a whole different ball game. I eventually stumbled along the corridor and found the right door, giving it a gentle knock and whispering 'Fridge, Fridge, Fridge' to try and get Colin to open up. He'd got the nickname after the American football player The Refrigerator, a nod towards Colin's deceptive strength.

After a few seconds the door swung open – and Craig Brown was standing there, wearing nothing but a towel. All sorts of things were running through my head, not least 'Why's the manager naked in my room?'. I was starting to wonder if there was more to Colin's call-up than met the eye.

Eventually Craig put me straight. I'd pitched up at the wrong room. He told me that he thought Colin and I were in the room directly below his and sent me on my way. At the second time of asking I managed to find the right room and found Colin had left the door slightly ajar. He was obviously expecting me back late. I made my way in towards my bed but before I got there I went crashing to the ground with the biggest thump you could imagine, ending up flat on my face. Fridge, it turned out, had pulled the retractable clothes line from the bathroom and tied it across the room like an SAS tripwire. God knows what Craig Brown made of it all. I always imagined him lying in bed above us, hearing the crash and thinking, 'That's Shearer into bed.'

I suppose you could argue the same sort of behaviour ended up getting Barry Ferguson and Alan McGregor banned from Scotland duty. On the other hand, the three of us had no chance of playing and we had our little session behind locked doors in Andy's room, well away from the public.

We certainly didn't do anything to hide it from the manager, either, and Craig was fine with it, even after getting woken up by me in the middle of the night. The next day at training he set me up good and proper, pulling me to one side with Alex Miller and telling me to fill Alex in with all the gory details of my attempts to get to bed. I started regaling Alex with tales of high jinks – and he blanked me completely, turned the other way and started shouting instructions at the other boys on the training field. Craig, knowing fine well that Alex would have been horrified by our exploits, just turned to me and smiled.

Alex certainly wouldn't have approved when John McGinlay and I pitched up late for a training session towards the end of the Euro 96 qualifiers. We'd already been with the squad for a couple of days when we were all given time off, with John and I heading north to Fort William for a night. The traffic on the way back was a nightmare and we couldn't make it back in time.

It was during that gathering that Craig took a group of us to one side on the training pitch and said he would be naming his squad for the last qualifier, against San Marino, in the next few days. He said that if any of us weren't involved and had any questions then we shouldn't hesitate to get on the phone to him and talk it over. I knew then and there that he was letting us down gently and that my name wouldn't be in that next squad list. My hunch was right and when the pool was named there was no place for me. In my absence, the boys won 5–0 to finish on a high and put us through to the finals in England as one of the best runners-up, with Russia winning the group by three points.

Obviously I was disappointed to have been dropped from the squad, but at the same time I always understood I had a role to play. I had been taken into the squad at a time when there were injuries to key players, particularly Ally McCoist. With Ally back in the frame and the likes of Gordon Durie forcing their way in, there was no room for me. I'd served my purpose and I could accept that. It would have been wonderful to have carried on through to the finals in 1996 but in my heart of hearts I knew it had come too late in my career.

What I will never be able to accept is any player turning his back on Scotland. I would have walked over hot coals to pull on that shirt and for the life of me I will never understand why people would take themselves out of contention. I've heard every excuse under the sun, but none of them wash with me. To play for Scotland should be the ultimate honour for any professional. Too many people apparently do not see it that way and it saddens me. 'Family reasons' is the one that's trotted out so often. Family reasons? I'm pretty sure if my father had been on his death bed he would have kicked me out the door to go and play for the national team – and that's exactly the way it should be.

I consider myself a very lucky man to have played for my country and scored a couple of goals. If I could have played on for another ten years at that level I would have gladly done so, but the decision was taken out of my hands. I never spat the dummy or went in the huff.

In fact, even after I'd played my last full international I was involved in a couple of B internationals and I had the same passion for those games as I did for the competitive ones. I captained the B team against Sweden in Stockholm in the autumn of 1995, with myself and Tom Brown scoring in a 2–1 win, and I classed that as a wonderful honour. I had never been a captain in professional sport and to lead out my country gave me a real buzz, particularly because it was Tommy Burns who made the decision to give me the armband.

Tommy was one of football's true gentlemen. I have never heard anyone say a bad word about him and there are very few people in the game that you can say that about. Tommy was a credit to his family and to Celtic Football Club and his death was devastating to all those who knew him. He was also a wonderful football man and an excellent coach, so working under him with the Scotland B squad, albeit briefly, was a pleasure. We travelled over with the A squad for the Sweden game and were playing on the night before the full international. Tommy came and tapped me on the shoulder while we were on the plane over and told me I would be captaining the team, which was a pleasant surprise to say the least. Craig Brown had asked me out to get some game time under my belt in case he needed me back in the main squad and it meant a lot that he and Tommy saw fit to give me the captaincy.

Winning and scoring was the icing on the cake and, with our part done, we were left to our own devices for the rest of the trip. After our B international, we had the following day in Stockholm to kill before the full side tackled Sweden later that night. Myself, Rab McKinnon and Brian Martin headed out to a bar near the hotel and ended up settling down for the afternoon sinking the biggest bottles of beer I've seen in my life. By the time kick-off in the main match rolled around it was all we could do to walk in a straight line to get on the bus to the game. I remember going down at half-time and getting chatting to some of the Tartan Army at the ground and sharing a few more drinks with them. After that it's all a bit hazy, but I believe it finished 2–0 to the hosts.

It was always business first and pleasure second, but once the hard work was out of the way it was never a problem to unwind with a few drinks. The only problem was when the young pups tried to keep up with the old dogs – and a few found to their cost that you have to know where to draw the line.

Jackie McNamara was one of those who fell by the wayside in spectacular fashion during one of the international trips, joining the squad for a B international against Denmark six months after that win we had in Sweden. Unfortunately, we got a real chasing that night, losing 3–0. Not surprisingly the mood wasn't exactly great but we headed back to the hotel and drowned our sorrows.

Someone came up with the bright idea of playing the drinking game 'Chase the Ace' and before long it was turning into a marathon session. It started with the whole squad involved but as night turned into morning there were more and more people dropping out.

Eventually it was down to me, John Robertson and wee Jackie. He was one of the youngsters in the squad, still in his early twenties, but should have known better than to try and match a Highlander and an honorary Highlander (as Robbo has become now he lives in the north) drink for drink. We'd started on shots of whisky but moved onto tequila and everything else under the sun before Jackie disappeared behind a big curtain and was horribly sick.

The next morning on the bus we found him with his face pressed up against the cold window trying to dull the pain of the night before. It might have done him a bit of damage in the short term but in the long run it didn't harm his chances. Jackie went on to make his debut for the full international side a few months later and stayed there for nearly a decade after that.

As he was starting out, I knew that my time with Scotland was over. I could have taken my fall out of the squad badly, but I never felt bitter. Instead, I dug out my Scotland scarf and joined the rest of the Tartan Army on the road south for Euro 96. It was a little bit odd to be sitting in the stands cheering on a squad that I had been part of less than a year before, but before long I was back to being just another supporter.

I wasn't alone, as it turned out. At the England game, after Paul Gascoigne's wonder goal, I turned on my heels to get out of Wembley. At the top of the stairs I bumped into John McGinlay, who had joined the masses in the Tartan Army for the big occasion. He must have thought the same as me when Gazza's shot hit the back of the net.

The atmosphere for that game was superb, as it was for the whole tournament. There was none of the nastiness I remember from Auld Enemy games when I was sixteen or seventeen years old. The banter with the England fans was great and, the result aside, it was a fantastic spectacle.

To be a fan is one thing, but to be a Scotland player is something else. I had great, great times with the national side and those memories will live with me forever. The time I spent with that jersey on my back meant far more to me than any contract I ever signed or pay cheque I banked. I know there are still players out there who have the same passion for the cause and it would be nice to think that the days of qualifying for major tournaments are not behind us.

15

THE END OF AN ERA

One of the most disappointing things for me was that Willie Miller never took another job in management after being sacked by Aberdeen in 1995. He is the man who caused me my biggest heartache in the game, when he came in and cleared out Steve Paterson and me from Pittodrie in 2004 after returning as director of football. Even now, with a lot of water under the bridge, I would question the validity of the director of football position at any club and whether it is the best use of a salary when playing staffs are stretched to the limit and budgets are being squeezed with every passing year.

As a manager, however, I could not fault him. The professionalism at Aberdeen under Willie was similar to the thoroughness at Blackburn under Kenny Dalglish, but on a smaller budget. Willie was methodical in everything he did, right down to his pre-match flip charts. I liked his approach and the detail he went into, particularly in team talks.

I only ever saw one man knock Willie off his stride and that was John Burridge. I'd played against Johnny often enough in England to know the type of character he was and when we signed him in 1994, in the midst of a goalkeeping crisis, I warned the rest of the boys that they wouldn't believe what they saw. He was a hell of a nice guy but totally unpredictable with it.

The routine at that time, for home games, was to report to Pittodrie for 1.30pm and then gather in the dressing room fifteen minutes later. For John's first game with the squad we all arrived as usual in our club blazers and ties and made our way through to our usual seats. No sooner had we got through than John started stripping down until he was totally nude, wearing nothing but his keeper's gloves.

We sat in the order of shirt numbers then, so the goalkeeper was always the first player and tucked away right behind the door as you came in the dressing room. Bang on schedule, at 1.45pm, Willie marched in with Roy Aitken by his side and started delivering the team talk. It wasn't until he was in full flow that he turned and clocked John, sitting there in his birthday suit. The place was in uproar. It's the most bizarre team talk I can remember.

John had come to Pittodrie in the 1993/94 season, the second campaign for me at the club and also Willie's second full term as manager. Having finished runners-up in all three competitions the year before, we went into the next season with high hopes of breaking Rangers' dominance – and there were signs that we could finally achieve that.

Things were evolving on and off the pitch, with the Richard Donald Stand (RDS) opening at the start of the 1993/94 season. Hamburg came over to play a friendly to mark the occasion, but the first competitive game in front of the new stand was against Clydebank in the League Cup. I scored a hat-trick in a 5–0 win and the noise from the RDS was fantastic. Having spent most of the previous season playing with nothing at the Beach End, apart from boards screening the construction work, it was brilliant to have Pittodrie back up to four stands. To look up to the top tier and see the fans bouncing around celebrating was a fantastic feeling.

My big thing was that I wanted to be the first to score in front of the RDS – but Alex McLeish beat me to it in the first game. He was hardly in the habit of scoring goals, but I couldn't berudge him it after everything he had done for the club over the years and all the times he had played in front of the old Beach End. I remember after his goal grabbing him and turning him round to face the stand and just saying to him 'look at that'. If I remember right, he replied with a few choice words. It was a phenomenal sight, a sea of red and white, with fans towering above us. That got the ball rolling and the new stand really did create a tremendous atmosphere – it was always a little bit more special for me when I scored in front of the RDS.

When I first went to Ibrox as an Aberdeen player, my breath was taken away by the noise generated inside the stadium. By building a big new stand, right on top of the players, we had given ourselves a fighting chance of generating the same type of intimidating atmosphere. Certainly that was the case in the early years, as the spirit grew among the supporters who made the RDS their new home.

It was after that game against Clydebank that the comparisons between myself and Joe Harper gathered pace, mainly because of Joey's tag as the King of the Beach End. A lot of the reporters had me dubbed as the King of the RDS or the new King of the Beach End, but I was quick to nip it in the bud. I remember telling the press that I didn't want to be remembered as the new anything, I'd rather make a name for myself by setting my own records.

In any case, I didn't want just one stand cheering – I wanted all four sides of the ground on their feet. In all seriousness, it was flattering to be compared to somebody with Joe Harper's record at Aberdeen. I was well aware of Joe's relationship with the supporters and although it wasn't something I tried to replicate, I was delighted that the fans responded so positively to me.

You often hear players say that you don't hear what's being shouted from the stands or what is going on around you. In truth, if you have a few thousand fans chanting your name or singing songs about you it's difficult to ignore and it does give you an extra spring in your step. Even towards the end of my time at Pittodrie, when I was out of the team and on the bench, there would be choruses of the songs ringing out from the stands and it is hard not to be touched by that type of affection.

The goals I scored certainly helped bring me closer to the fans, but I think the fact I was just an ordinary man doing a job I loved was another big part of the relationship I had with the Dons crowd. I hope they could see how much it meant to me to be playing for their club and the response I got certainly made it feel that way. As far as I was concerned I was one of them. The only difference was that I got to go on the park and play every weekend. I never set myself apart or had any high and mighty opinions of myself, so when the team went out for a few drinks on a Saturday night, I'd stay for one or two then go my own way. I didn't like to drink in the typical footballers' hangouts, the nightclubs and fancy bars. I far preferred finding a quiet, working man's pub, like the ones where I'd grown up in and around Caol. I made some great friends during my time in Aberdeen – people who took to me as Duncan Shearer the person rather than Duncan Shearer the football player. That was perfect for me.

I've been fortunate in my life to make a great living from football, but I've always considered myself working-class. I don't think I was ever in danger of getting carried away with fame or fortune – even if I had, there were plenty of friends and family around me who would have quickly cut me down to size.

It was different once I got out on the pitch, mind you. That was my domain and I became selfish in that environment. I often hear players, strikers particularly, saying they don't care who gets the goals as long as the team wins. I hate that. For me it was totally the opposite – I wanted the team to win *and* I wanted to score the goals.

It got me into trouble sometimes. I remember one game against Kilmarnock that we had won, but I wasn't happy because I hadn't scored and felt I should have done because of the positions I'd got myself into. I was having a real go at anyone who would listen and refused to go out for the warm-down because I was boiling with rage. Roy Aitken was furious with me and ready to dock my wages – I had one foot in the bath but decided to get my shoes back on and go out and join the fitness coach Stuart Hogg and the rest of the players back out on the park for the exercises.

When I look back now I realise I was throwing my toys out of the pram but that was the way I was. I wanted to score in every game. Don't get me wrong, I would still play other people in if they were in a better position but I saw my main job as scoring goals. I realised there were other people who could do other things better than me outside the box or who were more mobile but I always felt as a finisher I did okay and my good form continued into the 1993/94 season.

Going into the campaign we were taken away on a pre-season training camp in the Netherlands. We crossed over the border for a friendly in Germany against an amateur side – a game Theo ten Caat insisted would be all-out war. Theo kept saying he couldn't understand for the life of him why we were playing games like that.

He was right as well, it was a war. I was on the bench and dying to get on and into the trenches with the rest of the boys. I got the nod in the first half and pretty much my first involvement was to chase down one of the home players into the corner – getting the ball with one foot and then, with the old scissors move, lifting him off the ground with the other leg. It probably didn't help calm things down but it let him know we weren't going to roll over. It was a nightmare of a game but didn't do any harm with the team-building. It was one for all and all for one that day.

It was my first experience of pre-season abroad and, outbreaks of violence aside, it was a tremendous experience. To have the facilities and a bit of sunshine on our backs, with no distractions, gave us a great start. Even at Blackburn it had been a case of piling into cars to go to training, so the luxury in Holland was a pleasant change.

Stuart Hogg had been brought in to handle the fitness side of pre-season training and I loved his approach. He revised our training completely, with all of the running work done on the flat. It sounds obvious to say it, but football matches don't tend to be played on hills – yet team after team spends big chunks of the summer flogging players up and down hills.

Stuart recognised there was no sense in that and would lay out a 400m circuit to do timed laps on. After years in a culture that said a training session wasn't worthwhile until someone was being sick at the top of a slog up a hill, it was a breath of fresh air.

I went to the extent of getting copies of all of Stuart's pre-season training programmes and used them in later years at Caley Thistle and Aberdeen.

I still feel I was at my fittest while under Lou Macari at Swindon, but under Stuart's regime it was a happy medium in that I retained my power at the same time as building stamina. Under Lou I dipped as low as 12st, whereas with Aberdeen my playing weight was 13st 10lbs. When it came to weighing in on a Friday it was always a contest between Hugh Robertson and myself to see who was closer to the 14st mark. To be fair, most of that weight went into Shug's left foot – he had an incredible shot on him. People react differently to different approaches, but for me the training under Stuart was perfect and Willie's decision to bring him in was a good one.

We were fighting fit going into the 1993/94 season. In the league we pushed Walter Smith's team every step of the way, with some frustrating defeats against the likes of Hibs, Hearts and Partick proving our downfall. They were games we should have won and if we had then we would have won the league. Mind you, if we hadn't drawn twenty-one in the league then it would have been a different story. At the end of the forty-four-game marathon we lost out by just three points, with just six defeats along the way.

Although we had edged closer to Rangers in the Premier Division, we did not have the consolation of the cup final appearances that had given us hope the previous season. We lost 2–1 after extra-time against Rangers in the quarter-final of the League Cup and went out of the Scottish Cup at the hands of Dundee United after a replay.

Just as it had been at home, the European campaign was a case of 'so near, yet so far'. It was my first experience of playing at that level and I broke my duck when I scored in the first leg of the first-round tie against Valur in Iceland early in the season, a game we won 3–0 on our way to a 7–0 aggregate victory.

When Torino were pulled from the hat alongside us in the second-round draw there was a real buzz around the club and the city. I missed the first leg in Turin through injury, watching the drama unfold as we went down 3–2, but came back into the side for the return at Pittodrie. It was an incredible game to be involved in, with Lee Richardson's wonder goal the thing everyone remembers from it. To go down 2–1 at home was a real sickener because we had the measure of them that night. We had taken the lead in both legs but just couldn't hold out to go through.

In four competitions at home and abroad we had put up a real fight, but we finished empty-handed again. For the manager it was getting harder and harder to take, with more money invested in the summer of 1994 to try and take the team forward.

Billy Dodds, Colin Woodthorpe, Peter Hetherston and John Inglis were all brought in at a cost in excess of £1million and Stephen Glass was given his chance to shine. The first I knew about Billy's arrival was when Roy Aitken called me to tell me about the move. Maybe I should have been a little concerned that my place was under threat but I never feared competition and I thought it was a great signing. Roy hadn't called to get my opinion though, instead he wanted the shirt off my back. It turned out Billy had insisted he got the No. 10 jersey and since I had been wearing that number they needed to give me a heads-up. I've never been one for superstitions or rituals and I had absolutely no problem passing over the No. 10 to wee Billy – as I told Roy when he phoned to break the news to me, I'd score goals whatever top I was wearing. I knew Billy from our Chelsea days and was well aware of what he'd bring to the table, so I was looking forward to playing alongside him. I have kept in close contact with very few people in football, but Billy is one of those. Nicky Walker, another Pittodrie team-mate, is another I am still in touch with, as well as Colin Calderwood and Dean Windass.

I felt for Billy at the start of his time with Aberdeen because it didn't click straight away. He went through the sort of sticky patch that I had when I first went to Swindon and got some stick from the crowd, although all through that I think the supporters appreciated the amount of effort and energy he put into every game. Then the goals started flowing and he became a hero.

Billy's arrival at the start of the 1994/95 season added a new dimension, but the new recruits had a hard act to try and make up for the talent that left. We lost an awful lot of guile with the departure of Alex McLeish to Motherwell and the decision to allow Jim Bett and Robert Connor to move on. With those three gone and half a team introduced, it was sink or swim time for the manager's new-look team.

Unfortunately it just seemed to collapse around Willie in the 1994/95 season. The defeat in the UEFA Cup against Skonto Riga early in the campaign was a signal of things to come. After running Torino close the year before, the matches against the Latvians were the polar opposite. I played in the first leg over in Riga and it was a frustrating evening – we drew 0–0. That should have given us a good platform to finish the job back at Pittodrie but it didn't work out that way. I was on the bench, coming on in the latter stages, and it was a miserable game. A 1–1 draw was good enough for Skonto Riga to go through on the away goal rule and leave us licking our wounds.

They had arrived in Scotland for a bit of a holiday, not expecting to go through. All of their wives and girlfriends had come along for the trip and they spent the day shopping and seeing the sights in Aberdeen. Then they turned up at Pittodrie that night and dumped us out of Europe.

It was a shocking result and as we trudged off the park we were met by a line of photographers snapping away in our faces. There was a picture in the paper the next day of a group of three or four of us looking totally dejected and that image was trotted out again and again to illustrate the Riga result, with yours truly at the centre of it – even though I'd only played about ten minutes of the damn game. Mind you, we were all in it together and there was no getting away from how disappointing that match was for all of us.

We didn't think it could get any worse, but unfortunately it was just about to. The European form carried on into our domestic performances, although at the time I was helpless to do anything. I was kicking my heels on the sidelines because of the injury I'd picked up playing for Scotland in Finland just a few weeks into that season.

I was out for eight weeks after damaging my medial ligaments in September 1994. John Sharp, the Dons physio, was renowned for his rehab programmes and got me back ahead of schedule. I came back against Hibs in November, but just twenty minutes into the game my knee went again when Gordon Hunter, their big centre half, fell on top of my weakened leg. That was me again, out for another six weeks.

All I could do was sit and watch as we lost game after game, with just three wins on the board by the time we hit eighteen games and the halfway stage in the season at Christmas time in 1994.

When I made my second comeback of the season I was eased back in gently, coming off the bench against Hearts and then scoring a double in a 3–1 win against Hearts after starting in the next game. It turned out to be a flash in the pan, with just one other win in our next five games as the pressure began to mount.

Willie Miller was obviously a legendary player at Pittodrie, but that was not enough to protect him. Willie himself has admitted the strain of managing the club he had spent his entire career with was beginning to tell and maybe the board had to be cruel to be kind.

When the decision was taken to sack him it caught the players cold. I don't think any of us thought he would be dismissed and there was never any hint that he would walk away from the challenge either. That wasn't his style and after the near misses in the previous two seasons there were reasons to believe it could be turned around.

When you are a player you don't tend to get wrapped up in statistics or pay attention to the bad run the team is on. I discovered later in my career that it all changes when you are on the management side of the fence. Certainly while I was still playing, the only thing that I paid attention to was the next game, not the last one. At no point did I believe we couldn't get back on track. The only thing that suggested there was a threat to the manager was when the rumours began to spread that he had lost the dressing room.

Of course you would have to ask every individual player in

that squad, but speaking for myself, I simply don't believe that was the case. I always gave Willie my total respect – not because of anything he had done in the game; more because of the fact he was the boss. As far as I was concerned that mattered above all else.

The only thing I did see that concerned me was his treatment of some of the younger players. The likes of Stephen Wright, Scott Booth and Eoin Jess would get the full hair-dryer treatment, a trait Willie had presumably picked up from Sir Alex. I know from speaking to Jim Leighton and Neil Simpson that they had to put up with that in the glory days, but times change and in the 1990s that approach just didn't work. By then even the inexperienced boys knew their rights and how they should be treated . The bullying that had been commonplace just didn't fit in with the way the game was heading. The days when Jim McLean could pressure youngsters into signing ten-year contracts were long gone and similarly the days when kids could be terrified into playing better were also in the past.

I'd been in plenty of dressing rooms by then and seen managers do their share of shouting and swearing, but never in the way Willie would go face-to-face with certain players. You could see the fear in their eyes and I don't think it got the response it was designed to get. It was a shame because Willie was good at having a quiet word with players and giving their confidence a boost, but more often than not he'd choose to leave that side of things to Roy Aitken, while he played bad cop.

Despite that, we all expected he would be given time to turn things around. The directors did not see it that way and made their mind up to get rid of Willie while there was still time to move away from the relegation places. We had far too good a squad to go down, but that season we came within a whisker of dropping out of the top flight. It would have been ridiculous for a club of Aberdeen's stature to end up playing First Division football and I can only imagine that fear was what was playing on the minds of the board when they made their decision.

I turned up at Pittodrie on the morning of Willie's departure to be met by Andrew Shinie, who was Northsound Radio's sports reporter at the time. He asked me what I made of the news about Willie and I had to tell him that I had no idea what he was talking about. It gave me a clue about what was waiting for me inside, where all of the players were sitting around trying to digest the news that the manager had gone. By then Willie had been in, cleared out his stuff and disappeared. It was left to Roy Aitken to take training and try and pull us back together after what was a major shock.

He had been a big influence after coming to the club as Willie's assistant. With his pedigree and character it was a safe choice to hand control to Roy, although the decision also suggested that the board were not totally at odds with what Willie had been trying to do. After all, Roy had been a big part of that master-plan.

We went out and beat Rangers 2–0 at Pittodrie in Roy's first game in charge and it looked as though the traditional bounce from having a new man in charge was going to help us. Then it all went wrong.

We didn't think there was anything that could match the embarrassment of Skonto Riga – but Stenhousemuir had different ideas. We'd struggled past Stranraer in the third round of the Scottish Cup but nothing could prepare us for what Stenny had in store for us at Ochilview, where they beat us 2–0 to really pile the pressure on. It was absolutely horrific.

Tommy Steele is a name that will haunt me forever after what he did to us that day, scoring twice when we could have played for hours and not hit the back of the net. From the moment we arrived, driving through a big field to get to the back of the stand in pouring rain, there was a bad feeling about the tie. We had a midfield of Paul Kane, Joe Miller, Ray McKinnon and Eoin Jess on a park that was sodden and cutting up badly. All four of them liked to get the ball down and play but it was impossible on the surface underfoot and it went badly wrong. Plan B would have been to go long, get balls from back to front fired in towards me and get players up around me in support. We didn't revert to that, but in hindsight we probably should have done. In fairness to Roy, it would have been difficult to ask the midfielders to start lumping balls forward because it just wasn't in their nature.

We had a few chances. I remember Billy Dodds missing a glaring one, but nothing would fall for us and it was a quiet, quiet journey home. When we were sitting in the changing room at full-time there was no sign of the manager for a good five minutes after the whistle. When Roy did appear, he stuck his head round the door and said: 'Congratulations. You've just been part of the worst result in this club's history.' Then he was gone. He could have stood and ranted and raved for half an hour, but that one line said it all really.

There have been defeats since then that would probably rank as equally bad or even worse upsets – the likes of the Queen's Park defeat and more recently Queen of the South and Raith Rovers in the latter stages of the Scottish Cup – but I can honestly say I wouldn't wish it on anyone. A defeat like that brings stick from the supporters and the media, which is something you have to learn to live with. Let's face it, if I was a fan, paying good money to watch a club of Aberdeen's stature playing week in and week out, the very least I'd expect at the end of the season would be a cup final appearance to show for it. People talk about unrealistic expectations among Dons followers, but for me it is right that a club that size has ambitions to win trophies on a regular basis. When that doesn't happen then the players, the management and the directors can expect criticism.

Roy was cute in his approach in the aftermath of the

Stenhousemuir debacle and quite calculated. He gave the whole squad the day off on the Monday to reflect on what had happened and stew on the result. I decided to go into work anyway and was sitting having lunch on my own at Pittodrie when Roy pulled up a chair and had a good long chat with me. He told me then that the one thing that will follow you in football, and in life for that matter, is consistency. If you can find that in whatever field you're in then you will be successful. I took that advice to heart and it's something I have always strived for in my own efforts and looked for in others.

In that 1994/95 season there was nothing consistent about our performances or results. We were struggling down at the wrong end of the Premier Division table, we had gone out of the League Cup at the semi-final stage against Celtic, we had been humbled in Europe and then dumped out of the Scottish Cup by Second Division opposition. There wasn't one positive to take from it.

After that, the familiar pattern returned though and we toiled away at the bottom of the table. Fortunately, we hit form at the tail end of the campaign, winning the last three matches against Hearts, Dundee United and Falkirk. It was not enough to avoid the relegation play-off but it at least meant we could go into that two-legged contest with a measure of confidence.

It felt like the whole of the north-east was willing us to survive and the crowds around that time were unbelievable. In our hour of need, the Red Army came out in force. There were more than 20,000 in the ground for the penultimate league match against Dundee United and then against Dunfermline in the first leg of the play-off the stadium was packed to the rafters.

When we ran out at Pittodrie for the first leg of the play-off I knew there was no way we would lose. Had it not been for the incredible support that day then we may well have had a far more difficult time of it – but with a full house and a red-hot atmosphere, there was only ever going to be one winner. I scored a couple and Stephen Glass got one too to give us a 3–1 lead to take to East End Park. We won 3–1 down in Fife too, with Stephen scoring again and Billy Dodds on the score sheet along with Joe Miller to finish the job.

Those play-off games were tense affairs. I'd been involved in promotion play-offs in England that were absolutely massive but there's even more pressure when you're fighting for survival. We were so relieved when we came through that test and there was a realisation of just how close to disaster we had come. A repeat just wasn't an option.

16

FOOTBALL'S GREAT DIVIDE

In a perfect world you would have perfect harmony in every football dressing room the length and breadth of the country. I've been in a few squads where everything has been rosy in the garden but that scenario is very much the exception rather than the rule. More often than not there are obvious divides and Pittodrie was no different in that respect.

Just as you get clashes of personality in offices and factories, football clubs have their own tensions bubbling under the surface. Because you spend so long living in each others' pockets, the smallest things can get blown out of all proportion. When that happens, nobody wins.

The most brutal case I can remember involved John Inglis and Dean Windass when we were all together at Aberdeen. The bulk of the team had gone to a Professional Footballers' Association awards dinner in Glasgow in midweek and had stayed down in Glasgow for the night, travelling down in a fleet of cars before driving back up the next morning for training.

Deano had apparently said something on the journey down that had offended John and it had festered away for the rest of the night and into the next day. When we were back at Pittodrie, I caught the aftermath of the argument between the two of them. Dean was sitting on the treatment table in the middle of the changing room with blood gushing from his face and in a real sorry state. I wasn't there when it happened, but by all accounts he didn't stand a chance, and was caught unaware while he lay there on the table.

It was amazing that the club managed to keep it under wraps and that the press never got wind of what had happened. If they had, they would have had a field day and the club might have been forced to take more serious action than they did. As it happened it was kept in-house and the pair of them ended up being heavily fined and having their knuckles rapped, even though it was John who should surely have taken the biggest share of the blame.

I've no idea what Dean said to provoke that type of reaction from John, but whatever it was didn't merit the outcome. If John had a problem he should have been upfront about it and settled it face-to-face, rather than waiting until Dean was lying defenceless. The right thing to have done would have been to take it outside, away from everyone else, and had it out with Dean.

I let him know what I felt about the way he handled it and that he'd taken the coward's way out. I've never been a fighter, always preferring to talk my way out of situations, but if that's the way you want to settle scores then surely you do it the man's way and go toe-to-toe.

The funny thing in football is that for all the bravado, the ones who fancy themselves as hard men tend to be cowards. They will either jump on somebody when they are off-guard or they'll do it in front of a big crowd when they know that people will jump in and pull them apart before any real harm can be done. It's all for show as far as I'm concerned and the hardest players I've encountered have never been the ones to shout about it or make a big show of being tough. It's the quiet ones you have to watch and fear the most.

I've seen it happen a few times, but the bust-up between Dean and John was more serious than most. The only thing that came close was when the old West Ham forward Bobby Barnes went for Steve White during a training session at Swindon. Bobby waited until Steve was facing the other way before he pounced on him, giving him no chance of defending himself. Steve bided his time after that, picking his moment after another hard running session before he gave Bobby a real leathering. After the way Bobby had acted in the first place, nobody rushed in to separate them.

Mind you, at least the two of them didn't resort to name-calling. That was John Inglis' other little trick, hanging a 'Judas' sign on Brian Irvine's peg in the changing room after taking umbrage about something big Brian had written in his book, *What a Difference a Day Makes*. After everything he had been through, there was an interesting story to be told, but it was unusual in the sense that he was still playing when the book was published in 1996.

Brian is as honest as the day is long and he called things as he saw them. He had called into question the commitment of some of the west-coast players who were on the staff at Pittodrie at that time.

No names were mentioned, but it was obvious he was pointing a finger at the likes of John Inglis, Peter Hetherston and Billy Dodds. At that stage all three would shoot off down the road after training, not having relocated to the north-east after joining the club. For Brian, who had given his heart and soul to Aberdeen, it obviously touched a nerve that not everyone was as passionate about being part of it as he was.

John didn't see it that way and left that little sign for Brian when he came into work. It was like something out of primary school and came from someone who had done nothing in football compared to Brian, a man who had been part of a lot of success at club level and played for his country with distinction. If John had a problem with anything in the book he could have fronted things up, but that obviously wasn't his style. Brian was big enough to fight his own battles but to me the whole episode lacked any sort of class on John's part and certainly a real lack of courage. He certainly wasn't a 'Judas' or traitor, he had Aberdeen close to his heart and still does to this day.

Maybe by writing this book I'll offend a few people or touch a few nerves, just as Brian did with his own life story. I would argue that I'm entitled to my opinion, just as he was all those years ago. You have to be prepared to take criticism in football and I believe you should be able to be critical if you feel you have the justification.

Quite often I'm contacted by newspaper reporters who are looking for my thoughts on various issues surrounding the Dons. I will always be honest, no matter who it might upset, because I don't believe there is any benefit in tiptoeing around things that are being played out in a very public arena. For one thing, supporters are intelligent enough to know where the problems lie at any given time. Equally, if someone is doing something right they deserve to be praised and to enjoy their moment in the sun.

Unfortunately there are a few people in football who get wrapped up in everything going on around them and can't see the wood for the trees. They're happy to take the plaudits but not so keen on the criticism. Egos take over and you end up with players getting detached from reality.

I'll never forget turning up at Pittodrie in the build-up to the relegation play-off against Dunfermline in 1995 and finding queues of supporters snaking up the street as they waited to buy their tickets for the match. I was standing speaking to a few of the fans on the pavement when Paul Bernard came roaring down the road in his bright red sports car and pulled up in the car park opposite the main stand. There were hundreds of hard-working folk dipping into their pockets to lend support to a team deep in the mire, in danger of dropping out of the Premier League, and he was swanning around in a car worth more than a lot of people's houses. He might as well have driven down the street flicking two fingers up at them – it didn't matter whether Aberdeen were relegated or not, he'd still have his fancy car sitting in the driveway and a nice pay packet at the end of every month.

Don't get me wrong, what Paul or anyone else spent their wages on was none of my business. As I've said before, a player can only be paid what any club is willing to offer them and if cars are your thing then good luck to you. What I do think is that sometimes you have to be careful about the image you portray, and not least when it comes to the people who pay your wages by going through the gates week in and week out. Maybe that day, at a time when the team was struggling and he had barely kicked a ball for the club, he could have left the supercar at home and been a little more humble.

Cars have never really been my thing, so I have to admit I can't be sure which of Paul's cars it was. I do know that he got his hands on the Ferrari he'd always wanted when he was with Aberdeen, but it was just one of a clutch of sports cars he had during that period. Maybe he felt he had to live up to his tag as the club's record signing.

The fact that Aberdeen had spent £1million to sign Paul in 1995 was a sign of the way things were going at Pittodrie in the 1990s. As I mentioned previously, Willie Miller had invested heavily to take me back to Scotland and I was far from the only expensive signing he made.

Roy Aitken was also well supported by the board in the transfer market and the Bernard deal proved to be the peak of the spending. As we found out in the years that followed, it was money that the club really could not afford but there was a desperation to compete with the Old Firm on all fronts. The cash that was spent during that period, on the back of the big bill to build the Richard Donald Stand, remains a burden to this day and unfortunately the returns did not match the scale of the outlay. To talk of Aberdeen signing a £1million player now sounds like total fantasy – just imagine what that type of money could do for the playing budget now.

When I first heard we were signing Paul Bernard I thought he would be worth every penny of that £1million fee. I'd played against him when the Scotland team played our under-twenty-ones in a bounce match at Largs. He was powerful, never stopped running and picked the right pass every time. In short, he looked like the complete midfield player and every inch an international star in the making. He was still at Oldham then and it wasn't a surprise that he was attracting attention from other clubs, or that he went on to become a young international who looked to have a barrel-load of caps in front of him.

It should have been an inspired signing, but Paul suffered a hamstring injury early in his time at Aberdeen that caused him all sorts of difficulties. It wouldn't heal properly and was eventually traced to a back problem, but by then the damage had been done. He had been in and out of the side and never showed the quality that had won him the move in the first place.

Paul was just one of a glut of big-money men at around that time, with the Bulgarian pair of Ilian Kiriakov and Tzanko Zvetanov hoovering up at least a couple of thousand pounds a week during their time with the Dons. I had a lot of time for them, Tzanko especially, but it would be difficult to argue that they were at Aberdeen for the love of the club. At times it appeared as though Ilian loved his gambling, cigarettes and partying as much as his football.

He was a hell of a character and a tidy football player too, as you'd expect from somebody with World Cup experience. Judging by the stories they would tell about their time with the Bulgarian national team, he wasn't alone in taking full advantage of star status.

As talented as a lot of the expensive recruits undoubtedly were, I can't help but wonder what somebody like Brian Irvine must have made of it all. Along with Stewart McKimmie, he was one of the last remaining links to the Alex Ferguson era. All of that success had been built on a core of young, home-grown talent who would fight tooth and nail for Aberdeen Football Club. As time moved on, the emphasis shifted beyond all recognition and some of the soul was lost from the club. Now times are harder and money is tight, the hope is that things will get back to basics and it will be a love of the club and not money that motivates the next batch of players who pull on the jersey.

17

HAMPDEN GLORY

When Stewart McKimmie raised the League Cup above his head at Hampden on 26 November 1995, it marked the end of a five-year wait for a trophy for the Aberdeen supporters and an even lengthier pursuit of a winner's medal for me. I was thirty-three years old when we defeated Dundee 2–0 and I knew it could well be the last major final I played in. To have finally got my hands on silverware was wonderful, not least because I hadn't even expected to play in the game, and getting a goal in the final capped a memorable day.

The club had shelled out big money to sign Dean Windass in the summer, and I was pushed down the order by Roy Aitken and used mainly as an impact player from the bench. It turned out quite well in one respect because I scored a few goals. On the other hand it was incredibly frustrating, because no matter what I did I couldn't force my way back into the side. Billy Dodds and Dean went something like fourteen games without a goal, but there was still no recall for me.

In the run to the cup final I made just one substitute's appearance, coming on in the quarter-final win against Motherwell at Fir Park. All I could do was watch as we beat St Mirren in the second round, Falkirk in the third and then Rangers in the semi-final at Hampden. The match against Walter Smith's team was the one when Eoin Jess indulged in his little keepy-up display, and it put the Dons supporters into raptures. Eoin wasn't a show-off by nature but that day he was really on song and full of confidence. I still maintain that in a winning team and with his confidence high, there was no better player in Scotland than Eoin.

It was an injury to his sidekick, Scott Booth, that opened the door for me to play in the final back at the national stadium. The final was on a Sunday and it was during a training session at Pittodrie the day before that I first got wind of the news that I would be in the team. While we had a light session on the park there was a fitness test going on with Scott Booth.

Tommy Craig, who had been enlisted as Roy Aitken's assistant, whispered to me as we left the pitch that Scott wasn't going to make it. I said to Tommy: 'That's a real shame,' just managing to keep my smile in check. He knew exactly how I felt, not wishing ill on Scott but delighted that I was going to get my chance.

There were a few in the Pittodrie squad who clashed with Tommy but we always got on well and I learnt a lot when it came to coaching from him. Likewise, I enjoyed working with Drew Jarvie when he worked under Willie Miller and then Roy Aitken.

When Tommy came in to help Roy out, it took a period of adjustment. You had to adapt to his methods and his way of dealing with players. Peter Hetherston was one who made it clear he wasn't convinced and the pair of them had a real love-hate relationship. Peter, who had been brought in at the start of the season in which Willie lost his job, was the type who made his opinion heard and that led to plenty of interesting days on the training pitch when he and the assistant manager got going.

The thing with Tommy was that he was happy to listen if you approached it in the right way rather than trying to go at it hammer and tongs with him in front of everyone. On one occasion, when the team was going through a difficult spell, Tommy came to me and asked if there was anything he should be doing differently. I told him that for a start he could stop whistling for us as though we were dogs when it was time to start training – that was something that always annoyed me, but it was one of his habits when he was trying to round us up and get us out of the dressing room. Still, you can accept those little traits as long as you think the work you're doing on the training ground is worthwhile and in Tommy's case it was.

He appreciated that I always gave my all, whether I was in the team or not, and the cup final appearance was a reward for my perseverance that season. It was tough for Scott Booth to miss out, but an unexpected bonus for me to get a place in the starting eleven.

It was Billy Dodds and I up front for the match against Dundee. We had Michael Watt in goals, Stewart McKimmie, Stephen Glass, John Inglis and Gary Smith at the back and a midfield of Brian Grant, Paul Bernard, Joe Miller and Eoin Jess.

Dundee had been going well in the First Division under Jim Duffy that season, only beaten once in the league, and that was in a derby against Dundee United early on in the campaign. In the game before they played us they made up for that by beating United 3–2 in the rematch at Tannadice, so they were on a real high. In their run to the final, Dundee had put Hearts out in the quarter-finals and overcome a tricky tie against Airdrie in the semis to earn their place at Hampden.

There were some real talents in Jim's team at that stage, players who were obviously destined for a bigger stage. Morten Weighorst, the Danish international who went on to play for Celtic, was always a tough customer and Neil McCann on the wing was emerging as one to watch.

Despite their good run and decent squad – not to mention what had happened to us at Stenhousemuir the previous season – I don't think any of us even contemplated losing to Dundee in that final. With a cup on the line there was only going to be one winner. We had been underdogs against Rangers in my previous two cup finals, even if we didn't see it that way going into those games, but this time we were the overwhelming favourites and we had to be confident.

Still, it was clear we would need an early goal to set us on the way and Billy Dodds came up with the goods. When I nicked the second just after the break it was time to soak up the occasion and start looking forward to the celebrations. After I scored that second goal I had the most rousing reception I've ever had from a football crowd, helped in no small part by the fact Jim Duffy and another of his Dundee colleagues had collided as they tried to stop me tucking the ball away. They both went down needing treatment and were on the deck for a good three or four minutes. In the meantime, we were back in position waiting for Dundee to kick off and all that time the Aberdeen supporters were on their feet singing the song that they had adapted to the tune of 'Winter Wonderland'.

'It's a goal, Duncan Shearer, It's a goal, Duncan Shearer, Walking along, singing a song, Walking in a Shearer Wonderland' was being belted out from the Hampden stands in perfect harmony, while Billy Dodds and I stood on the edge of the centre circle. Billy turned to me and said: 'Are you the only player in this team?' It felt like that at times with the support I had from the fans, not just with that song but with the other chants they used to direct towards me.

Even now, when I have the occasional night out in the pubs around Aberdeen, it doesn't take long for the 'Wonderland' song to be struck up. I've always felt very fortunate to have had that type of relationship with the Dons fans. It meant a lot to me when I was playing and I still value it now. I've seen the other side of the coin, when I was jeered by the crowd at Swindon in my early days there, and maybe that made me appreciate the warmth of the Aberdeen faithful even more.

It wasn't a bad performance that day, with Stephen Glass among those who shone, and the struggles of the previous campaign felt like a distant memory when the full-time whistle went and the cup was handed over.

Having missed the open-top bus parade when Swindon won promotion, there was no way I was going to make the same mistake again. I didn't expect too many people to venture out in the middle of winter to welcome us home but in fact there were thousands lining the streets and it was a great experience to come back to Aberdeen with a trophy for the fans.

What nobody anticipated was that it would be the last cup to be placed in the Pittodrie cabinet for more than fifteen years. Given that one of the previous managers, Alex Smith, had been sacked even after winning two cups, it would have been unbelievable at that time to think of going more than a couple of years without success. There was real pressure to deliver, but over the years there's been an unfortunate acceptance that the days of regular wins in the big competition are gone. It would be lovely to think that Aberdeen will soon be back on the big stage year in and year out – it is no less than the supporters deserve.

Good runs in the cup competitions have a knock-on effect in the league and after beating Dundee we put the relegation worries of the last season behind us, going on to finish third behind the Old Firm. Celtic pushed Rangers all the way in that 1995/96 term and the two of them stretched away from the rest of the pack. We were at the top of the pile beneath the Glasgow two, just pipping Hearts to third place. With pride restored in the Premier Division, a cup in the board room and a place in the UEFA Cup guaranteed it was a great first season for Roy.

Personally I had had a decent year. At my age I accepted I wouldn't start every match, albeit grudgingly, and I played in the majority of games in one way or another. Half of my thirty appearances in the league were from the bench and I featured in some of the big cup ties too, with the goal in the cup final against Dundee obviously the highlight and another goal in the Scottish Cup semi-final against Hearts not enough to save us from going down 2–1.

That summer I found myself out of contract and in among a group of experienced members of the squad that the manager had to make a decision on. They were keen to get together and go knocking on Roy's door to see what the score was, but I'd never asked for a contract in my life and said if he wanted to keep me he knew where I'd be.

I was relaxed about the situation. By then Alex McLeish had taken charge at Motherwell and I had an inkling that he would have taken me to Fir Park if I hadn't stayed at Aberdeen. As it happened, Roy came to me and offered me a new deal. There was no signing-on fee but a good appearance bonus, which felt like a great deal at the time. Without hesitation I decided to stay with Aberdeen for the 1996/97 season.

The preparations didn't exactly go smoothly. The pre-season trip to the Continent ended in chaos when the group dubbed the 'Austrian Six' got collared for an illicit night out on the town. The day in question had begun pretty normally, with a training session at our base for the camp in Seefeld. I had a big bust-up with John Inglis during the afternoon and after we'd eaten I went through to the players' lounge area to watch a film. Billy Dodds joined me and when John came through to ask if the pair of us were heading out for a walk with the rest of the boys it was a flat 'no' from me. He asked if I was still in a huff and the answer to that was definitely 'yes'. He stomped out of the room, cursing us, and obviously then went and rounded up the rest of the troops.

Billy decided to stay with me while John and a group of the players headed into town for a look around. They ended up in a café and as the night wore on, found out that there was a night-club underneath. As more and more of the locals piled in, the Aberdeen crew decided to head downstairs and investigate the local nightlife. One thing led to another and they ended up spending the night sampling the Austrian lager before staggering back up the road to the team hotel in the wee small hours.

Roy Aitken and Tommy Craig were away scouting and had left Stuart Hogg and David Wylie, the physio, back at base to keep an eye on things. Stuart was apparently going spare as he sat in the foyer of the hotel waiting for the AWOL group to come back. It was near enough 4am by the time they did. Bearing in mind we had a game later that day, against the Greek side Xanthi, it wasn't exactly model professionalism.

When Roy came back and discovered what had been going on, he went through the roof. Understandably, he was absolutely raging and he clobbered all of the offenders with massive fines. I think it cost each of them £2,000 and between them they helped pay for a big chunk of the cost of that summer's tour. All the time Billy and I were sitting smugly watching the rest of them getting a mauling, enjoying the fact we'd had the good sense to give the night out a wide berth.

Any hope of keeping it quiet was dashed when somebody leaked details to the *Daily Record* and the Austrian Six ended up splashed across the next day's paper. Stewart McKimmie, Ilian Kiriakov, Brian Grant, Dean Windass, John Inglis and Paul Bernard were the ones who were named and shamed. In that bunch you had the club captain in Stewart, the new recruit in Ilian and the most expensive player in Paul.

It was a great story for the papers and it wasn't just the players who were on the receiving end of a telling off. The young *Evening Express* reporter got it in the neck from his editor too after being scooped by the *Record*, despite the fact he was out in Austria with the team. The mistake he made was going to bed at a decent hour when he should have been out in the pub with the drinkers. You live and learn.

Part of Roy's punishment for the sinful six was to make them play in that day's game against the Greeks. I was fuming, sitting on the bench while the rest of them got to play, but I could see his logic. They were run ragged, struggling to keep up with the opposition, and we were beaten 3–0 to prove the manager's point.

Some of the six took it harder than others. I found Stewart McKimmie, who was still captain at that point, sitting ashen-faced in the airport as we waited to fly home. He was tossing his mobile phone from hand to hand, trying to build up the courage to phone his wife. By then she would have read all about it in the papers anyway, but Stewart was on a tight leash at home and was obviously fearing he was about to get another ear-bashing after the one he'd got from Roy. On the other hand, when I called Michele the first thing she asked was: 'Why weren't you there? And where was Billy when all of this was going on?' She was more suspicious of the fact the two of us had missed out on a good night out than anything else.

I may have got a few brownie points at home with my good behaviour on tour, but it didn't do me too much good in the long term at Pittodrie. I quickly discovered that I wouldn't be picking up too many of the appearance bonuses Roy had offered me at the start of the summer.

He had taken the decision to give youth its chance and, to be brutally honest, I couldn't understand the logic in moving those players ahead of me. Michael Craig was one of them and while he was a good player it was obvious he was too lightweight for the Premier Division. Malcolm Kpedekpo was another who got game time ahead of me and it even extended to reserve games, where Roy decided it was better to give the kids a chance to play rather than have me taking up a place in the second string when he already knew what I could do. Because of that I could go four or five weeks without a game and at my age it was difficult to keep match fit in those circumstances. I did plenty of running and fitness work with Stuart Hogg but there was nothing like competitive games.

I still managed to rack up more than thirty appearances, with the bulk from the bench, but I would be thirty-five when the 1997/98 season got into full flow and I knew the clock was ticking for me at Aberdeen. Just a month or so into that campaign, in September 1997, Roy called me into his office and told me that there had been some interest from other teams.

Motherwell, still managed by Alex McLeish at that stage, wanted to sign me but Roy told me the club wasn't keen to let me go to Fir Park. I found that incredible given I wasn't getting a look-in at Pittodrie but I was still under contract and ultimately it was their decision. During that conversation the manager also told me there was something else that might interest me – an approach from Caley Thistle about a role as player-coach.

They were in the Second Division at that time and it suited Roy better to have me drop down a couple of leagues rather than have the prospect of me coming back to play against his side with Motherwell or another Premier Division side. I later found out that Alex McLeish had even tried to take me on loan to Lanarkshire when I was kicking my heels on the sidelines, but Roy had turned that down point-blank, so there was no way he was going to let me away permanently to a top-flight side.

I went away and discussed the situation with Michele and we both agreed that the Inverness opportunity was one worth exploring. My playing days were coming to an end and moving into coaching was something I had always planned, having completed my qualifications while at Pittodrie. The chance had come out of the blue but it was one that made sense. From a personal perspective, getting back to the Highlands was a big lure after so long away, and I had a great affinity with Inverness from my Clach days.

Roy gave me permission to speak to Caley Thistle and I travelled up to Steve Paterson's house at Garmouth. Steve greeted me by telling me: 'Duncan, I'll be honest with you and admit I've got absolutely nothing to do with any of this – but I'll be delighted if it works out.' It turned out that the transfer was the work of the club chairman Dougie McGilvray.

Dougie had big ambitions to take the club into the SPL by the year 2000 and his enthusiasm was infectious. He turned up at Steve's house and between the three of us we thrashed out a deal that offered me the best of both worlds, with a part-time playing contract, in keeping with the rest of the squad at that time, and another part-time job heading up the club's youth development programme. Those two combined gave me a decent wage and although it didn't come close to the pay I was on at Aberdeen it did offer the security of a three-year contract. At that stage in my life, that type of stability was a real plus for me and the whole vibe I got from that meeting with Steve and Dougie felt right.

Caley Thistle had won the Third Division the previous season and, after all the acrimony and challenges of the merger between Caledonian and Thistle, there was a lot of momentum building to win a place in the Scottish Football League. Although the youth system was nothing like as comprehensive as it is today, there was still plenty to keep me busy on that side and the combination of the two appeared ideal.

I made my decision pretty much then and there, but soon discovered it wasn't going to be an easy path. I went back to Pittodrie to tell Roy that I planned to move on and he said 'no problem'. A day or two went past and I still hadn't heard anything more or had any further contact from Inverness, so I phoned Dougie McGilvray – who told me the deal was dead in the water.

Aberdeen had suddenly turned round and demanded a £15,000 transfer fee. Dougie explained that if they had to pay that sort of money then it would eat into what they could pay me in wages, so there was no way it could be done.

I was raging. Roy Aitken was impossible not to like – he was such a bubbly and enthusiastic character – but the way he had handled the situation infuriated me. I went back to him and let him know exactly how I was feeling. After the service I'd given Aberdeen and the goals I'd scored, I felt I deserved better. After all, he'd been happy enough to let Stewart McKimmie, Brian Irvine and a few other senior players walk away for nothing and he'd given the impression I would be treated in the same way. It wasn't as though I was in his plans for the first team and I thought it was out of order. Roy came back to me pretty quickly and said I was free to go, presumably after a call to Stewart Milne. Whether it was Roy or the chairman, it was obvious someone thought they could make a quick buck and squeeze a decent sum out of Caley Thistle. What Aberdeen had to remember was I could have sat out my contract and picked up my wages for another year, which financially would have made perfect sense for me, so I was saving them a decent amount by agreeing to move on early.

All that was left to do after finally getting the transfer ironed out was to go back to Pittodrie to say my goodbyes and collect my boots before heading back north to get started with Caley Thistle. I left having made some great friends and with amazing memories but all good things come to an end and it was the right time for a fresh challenge.

18

HIGHLAND HOMECOMING

Almost fifteen years after leaving Clach to join Chelsea, I found myself going full circle and back playing part-time football in Inverness. It felt like I was going home in a sense and it was exciting to be back on familiar territory to play a part in establishing Caley Thistle as a force in the senior game.

I knew as well as most how bitter the rivalry between Inverness Caledonian and Inverness Thistle had been, and the merger of the two had obviously been contentious. At the same time it had created a wonderful opportunity for the north to get a foothold in a game that for too long had been dominated by teams in the central belt. I think the events in the sixteen years since Caley Thistle were born have proved that the club deserves its place at the highest level.

When I first arrived in 1997, the idea of upsetting the Old Firm and playing in the SPL felt like a distant dream. Yes, that was the grand plan in the boardroom but we all knew that turning that into reality would be a long and difficult process.

My first game was at home to Stranraer and I scored within six minutes or so, keeping up my good record of finding the net on all but one of my debuts. It was great to get off on the right footing – but even after that first game I had a few doubts about what lay ahead. There was just the one stand at the stadium in those days and it was a bit eerie running out in front of 1,500 people when I'd been used to big games at the likes of Pittodrie, Hampden, Ibrox and Parkhead with Aberdeen. It felt like there was nobody there and even after that first game I was thinking to myself, 'I've dropped down too far.'

The team back then was a combination of players from all types of background. There were those who had been around the senior game, in the shape of Barry Wilson and Paul Cherry, as well as those plundered from the Highland League like Charlie Christie, Iain Stewart, Davie Ross and Brian Thomson. Steve also had a couple of emerging young players coming into the team, with Richard Hastings just beginning to make his mark on his way to becoming an international player with Canada.

We came together for training at school playing fields on Tuesday and Thursday evenings at 7pm, with a lot of the players dashing straight from work to make it in time. It was a shock to the system for me and I quickly discovered that part-time football was going to be tough. Going back to training a couple of nights a week for the first time since I left Clach took a lot of getting used to. I'd try to keep myself ticking over by running laps round the track, but when you're out there on your own there's not the same edge as when you're working in a group.

I plugged away and chipped in with a few goals in a season that was one of consolidation in the Second Division, finishing mid-table in 1997/98. The next season I was still involved as we won promotion to First Division, finishing runners-up to Livingston, and I made it into double figures with thirteen goals. We were just five points behind Livi and they were emerging as our big rivals, with similar ambitions to reach the top league and with the same 'new' feel to the club. At that stage Ross County were a division behind us, so it was a few years before the Highland derbies came back on the agenda.

Livingston were throwing money at their attempt to plough through the leagues, while Caley Thistle had to be a lot cleverer, picking up players that other clubs had discarded and building a team with some brilliant characters. There was a real buzz around Inverness after our promotion success and I would have loved to have played a big part in the First Division effort, but I knew time was catching up with me. Stepping up a league, in among full-time sides like St Mirren, Falkirk and Dunfermline, was going to be difficult for me at the age of thirty-seven.

I accepted that and Steve Paterson could obviously see it too, although it was difficult for him. I played in a few of the First Division matches before he sat me down one day and told me he was leaving me out of the team to make way for fresher legs. Steve was apologetic about it, but he didn't have to be. He was right and there was no argument from me – although judging from his relief, he must have been expecting one. He was building for the future and in that 1999/2000 season he managed to get a foothold in the First Division, finishing sixth and proving that Caley Thistle belonged at that level.

After the meeting with Steve, I went home that night and told Michele that I thought I'd come to the end of the road as far as playing was concerned. There were no tears or anger, I'd had a good run in the game and been very fortunate to have avoided any serious injuries that would have taken the decision out of my own hands. There are a lot of players who do not have a decision to make because a doctor makes it for them and I was glad to be able to take a step back and wind down on my own terms.

It wasn't just events on the park that influenced my decision. I was beginning to come under a bit of scrutiny for the wages I was rumoured to be picking up at Caley Thistle and the last thing I wanted to do was cause any unrest among what was a really tight-knit squad. The average wage would have been no more than £400, yet there were stories coming out that I was earning way above the rest of the players.

The truth was somewhere between that figure and some of the wilder rumours about my salary. Given that I was doing two jobs, with the youth development role as well as the playing commitments, it was an honest wage. Not everyone saw it that way. It all came to a head when the journalist and author Hugh Dan Maclennan wrote what I felt was a fairly vicious newspaper article about me, criticising what he claimed was a £1,000 weekly wage for playing a game of which he was never the biggest fan. The thing that hurt the most was that Hugh Dan didn't have the decency even to call me to try and establish the facts or argue the toss with me before he wrote the piece. That was all the more galling since we'd grown up as neighbours, with my football going over his fence and shinty sticks being thrown back in return. Shinty was always Hugh Dan's game and maybe that was behind what I saw as an attack on me by someone I considered a friend. I'd even spoken at the launch of one of his shinty books, but he obviously had his reasons for writing the things he did.

It seemed like people were questioning my contribution and that wasn't fair on the manager or the club, so the sensible thing to do was take a step back from playing. I was already getting more involved in coaching at Caley Thistle by that point. I made the occasional appearance when Steve needed me, playing my last competitive game at the grand old age of thirty-eight, when we drew 1–1 with Clyde at Broadwood in November 2000. But I'd made my mind up that I'd throw all of my energy into coaching. I didn't know where that would take me and couldn't have predicted the highs and lows that would follow.

19

POACHER TURNED GAMEKEEPER

One of the best pieces of advice I ever had as a coach was that learning the job is no different from being taught to drive a car. You go through the lessons and do everything by the book, then once you've passed your test you can do it your own way. It was Andy Roxburgh who made that point, when he was putting me through the SFA coaching badges at Largs, and I knew exactly what he meant.

The criticism of the Largs Mafia over the years has become almost a running joke in Scottish football. All those preconceptions about the training courses run by the SFA are based on the mistaken idea that everyone who goes through the system sticks to the manual, just like a learner driver abides by the Highway Code. That may be the case for one in every ten coaches passing through Largs – but for the vast majority, including myself, the qualifications are simply the foundation for building your own approach to coaching.

When I look back at my own start in the game as a kid in Lochaber, I don't remember ever being coached as such. There'd be somebody on the touchline with a bag of oranges, but that was about the extent of it. Mostly we were self-taught, either from playing morning, noon and night, or from battering a ball off a wall for hours on end.

I went back to my roots when I returned to Caley Thistle in

2008 to work with the club's under-fifteen players, a role I'm still in today. It's a vital stage in their development and they want to learn – but sometimes I'll say to them, 'Right, we're just playing football tonight.' No drills, no tactics, just football. There has to be a chance to go out and enjoy the game, the way we used to on the streets and in the parks. It's a different world now because the kids just don't have the same time to develop in that natural way, so there has to be structure to the coaching, to teach them all the things that decades ago would have become second nature from just playing the game. At the same time, there has to be freedom to express themselves built into it.

I went through my coaching badges at the same time as Brian Irvine and Brian Grant while I was still at Aberdeen, starting out more than fifteen years ago. In that time I've been learning with every day and night spent on the training ground and it's not the type of job where you can ever sit back and think you know it all. The game is changing all the time and coaches have to move with it.

We had great fun doing the qualifications, starting with the B Licence then the A Introductory and A Advanced Licences. I also went on to complete my youth diploma and that has been a big bonus for me and Caley Thistle, since every club requires two coaches with that certificate to qualify for the full youth development grant from the SFA. Not having those fully qualified members of staff can cost a significant amount each year in lost funding but myself and Charlie Christie fulfil the criteria for Inverness. We also have the ten coaches with the SFA Youth Level 4 qualification to ensure we receive the full financial backing.

When I first joined Caley Thistle in 1997 we had under-twelve, under-thirteen and under-fourteen teams. That has expanded in both directions and now we start as young as under-ten and, following the return to the SPL in 2010, right the way up to under-nineteen level. In the 1990s there was no organised league structure and we took games wherever and whenever we could. Now we are in the performance structure and playing against fellow SPL teams on a weekly basis, something that helps bring our players on in leaps and bounds.

I get as much satisfaction from my current job, working with the up-and-coming young players, as I do from working with senior players. It takes very different skills to deal with those different groups and it was under Steve Paterson that I began to get more involved with first-team coaching.

When I arrived at the club it was Alex Caldwell who assisted Stevie. When we made the transition from part-time to full-time football it became more and more difficult for Alex, who was trying to combine his coaching commitments with his job with a courier company in Inverness. He'd do an early-morning shift and then come into work at the club looking absolutely shattered, with Steve often telling him to go home and get some rest. By default, that opened the door for me to start leading some of the training sessions and I built up a good rapport with the players, something which must have been hard for Alex to take.

When he got the chance to manage Elgin City early in 2000 it was too good an opportunity to miss. That was when I got the invitation to step up and become assistant manager to Stevie.

My first game in my new job was very nearly the biggest – the Scottish Cup win against Celtic at Parkhead. I was officially due to start work on Monday, 7 February and on Tuesday, 8 February – a date that is etched in the memory of everyone connected with Caley Thistle – we humbled the Hoops in their own back yard. But instead of taking my place in the dugout alongside Stevie, I was sat in the stand alongside our reserve coach John Docherty.

Alex Caldwell had agreed to take the Elgin job even before the draw had been made, but always intended to sign off after the next round of the cup, which just happened to be Celtic away.

We went down there on the Saturday to discover part of the guttering hanging off above the stand and with high winds whipping around the ground there was no way the game could be played. It was a blow for us because we'd built up to that day, but it was the right decision in the circumstances. At that point Alex should have walked off into the sunset and left me to take over but he took the decision to hold on until the replay.

I was champing at the bit but Stevie had to let me down gently and tell me I wouldn't be taking over the job until after the tie. I was disappointed, of course I was, but I didn't begrudge Alex that last game – and what a match it was.

We had prepared as best we could, but we never once spoke about going down to Celtic Park realistically expecting to win. Sitting in that stadium, I couldn't believe what I was watching. We didn't just beat Celtic that night, we annihilated them. I'd played at Parkhead plenty of times with Aberdeen and had some decent results but nothing on a par with the performance that particular night. To go down to Glasgow and beat them 3–1 in their own back yard was incredible. When Barry Wilson scored early on, the celebrations were short-lived because Mark Burchill went up the other end and equalised. Lubomir Moravcik's own goal put us back in front and then of course Paul Sheerin kept his cool from the penalty spot to give us that extra cushion at 3–1 in the second half.

The only fear, sitting there watching it, was that Ian Wright was on the bench. I'd played against Ian and knew the threat he could pose and when he got the nod to come on there was a part of me that feared he could turn out to be Celtic's hero. In the end, he faffed around like all of the rest of his team-mates. I can remember turning to John Docherty as the clock ticked down, with both of us thinking the same thing, and saying: 'This is really going to happen.'

While it was difficult being away from the frontline on the night, I still felt part of it. A lot of the players paid tribute to our preparation for the match in the post-match interviews and spoke about the role Steve, Alex and I had had. For me that was enough to make it all worthwhile.

We had tried to keep the build-up as normal as possible. We travelled down on the day of the game rather than staying overnight in Glasgow and it was always Steve's philosophy that players performed better if they had a good night's sleep in their own bed rather than in a hotel room miles from home. The results proved the theory, with some great performances on the back of long road trips and some thumpings at the likes of Queen of the South after overnight stops.

We approached playing Celtic exactly as we would have approached playing Morton – it was just the reaction to the win that was a little bit different. The celebrations went on and on, starting at Parkhead. There is a private players' lounge with a free bar at Celtic and we ran it dry that night. I had a conversation with Paul Lambert in there and he said to me: 'Duncan, there will be repercussions from this.' I didn't understand the extent of those repercussions at that point, but Paul obviously had an inkling of what lay ahead for John Barnes. The speed with which the manager was removed from his post was incredible, but I think the manner in which they were beaten meant there was no way back for him.

To be fair to Celtic, they did not take their frustration out on us. Even when we were sitting on the team bus ready to head up the road, some of the staff came out to catch us and pass a couple of crates of beer on board. We headed to a hotel at Bridge of Allan before driving back to Inverness.

Stevie, Barry Wilson and Charlie Christie came back to my house and we sat up until 4am still trying to take in what had happened. Nobody deserved more praise than Charlie after what had been a marvellous performance against his old club. He was outstanding – though that was no surprise to anyone in Inverness.

Training had been cancelled on the Thursday and the party moved from my place to the Fairways Golf Club for breakfast and a few more beers. The phones were ringing off the hook but we were happy enough to lay low and soak it all up.

In hindsight it would have been sensible to put a few bob on St Mirren to win when we played them that weekend because nobody was in great shape. Sure enough, we were turned over and it was very much a case of 'after the Lord Mayor's show'.

I don't think the Celtic result was a fluke though. The team we had was something special – the type that only comes along once in a blue moon. We had assembled a group of players who were not well-paid and were not particularly well-known but boy could they play the game the right way.

Steve Paterson had a great ability to spot a player and he also knew how to listen to the opinions of people around him before making a judgement.

Bobby Mann was a case in point. Bobby is the best football-playing centre-half I have ever played alongside. In terms of his vision, passing ability and reading of the game he was well ahead of internationals like Colin Hendry and Colin Calderwood, or even Premiership veterans like Kevin Moran. Yet he was playing for Forfar when Steve signed him for Caley Thistle and he probably wouldn't have made the offer if it hadn't been for Iain Stewart's insistence. Iain, who was scoring goals for fun for Inverness, maintained Bobby was his worst night-mare to play against – he read Iain's every move. He said he'd far rather be on the same side as Bobby than against him and Steve made it happen. Bobby went on to become a fantastic captain and player for Caley Thistle and when Steve and I went to Aberdeen we swithered about taking him with us to Pittodrie. The only thing that put us off was the concern that there would be big question marks about his fitness. We didn't view it as a problem but knew that if it didn't work out then it would be the first thing that people would point a finger at. Bobby's body shape is the only thing that prevented him playing at the highest level.

We could forgive the odd flaw in a player as long as they fitted with what we were trying to achieve with the team. In a way, we saw it as our job to mend the characters and players who, for whatever reason, had struggled at their previous clubs.

Barry Robson is an obvious example. My first recollection of Barry is watching him playing for the Rangers youth team against the Aberdeen kids at New Advocates Park, just a stone's throw from Pittodrie. He spent most of the match moaning and sulking, the moodiest little so-and-so I'd ever clapped eyes on. John Brown and John McGregor on the Rangers touchline spent the entire ninety minutes tearing their hair out and arguing with him. Barry was everything that was wrong about a football player in terms of attitude but at the same time I could see he had enough to make up for it. He had ability but he also had a nasty streak and a will to win that set him apart from every other teenager on the park that day. When we heard he was available on a free transfer from Rangers we had to have him. He would know better than me, but I'd imagine that deep down he views those seasons at Caley Thistle as wasted years. I've no doubt he enjoyed them at the time – we all did – but Barry will know that he should have been playing at a far higher level than the First Division. It wasn't a real surprise when he did so well at Dundee United and got his move to Celtic and I'm convinced he'll make just as big an impact in England with Middlesbrough.

Barry was typical of the type of player that Caley Thistle picked up at that time. There wasn't a big budget to work with but we could offer regular first-team football and the chance for players who had been unwanted elsewhere to prove people wrong.

When I moved north from Aberdeen in 1997, Steve picked my brains about the fringe players at Pittodrie. Straight away I picked out Denis Wyness as one he had to go after. I'd watched Denis at close quarters coming through the ranks at Aberdeen and was a huge admirer of his touch and vision. The only thing he lacked was the touch of aggression that the very best strikers have. As expected, he found himself surplus to requirements at the Dons and we made a move for him. Then suddenly a £15,000 price tag was hung round his neck. I told Steve that it would be the best £15,000 he'd ever spend and to his credit he pushed the boat out to get the deal done.

Russell Duncan was another player shown the door by Aberdeen and picked up by Stevie. More than nine years on, Russell is still doing the business for the club in the quiet but effective way that has made him a fixture in the team under a succession of managers.

All of those players came together wonderfully and I don't think there's ever been a team like it at the level we were at. To this day I get people stopping me to tell me how much they enjoyed watching our games back then and even normally impartial reporters have said it is the only side they would have paid to watch.

It was total football, with the ball rolled out from the goalkeeper for big Bobby to build from the back. With Barry Robson on one wing, Barry Wilson on the other and Charlie Christie pulling the strings in the middle of the park, there were players right the way through to the likes of Denis and then Paul Ritchie up top. Steve wanted the style of play to be totally pure and wouldn't compromise.

I can only ever remember one deviation from that vision. It came ahead of a Scottish Cup tie against Ayr United early in 2001 when Stevie announced on the Friday that he wanted to do things differently. We'd sit down after training every Friday, usually with John Docherty, and run through the plan for the following day's game. On this occasion Steve said he wanted to do it a particular way, obviously wary of an Ayr side who were going very well under Gordon Dalziel at the time.

He went through it all in great detail, marking it down on the board, and on paper I couldn't disagree with what he had in mind. Then we were sitting having a cup of tea at 1.30pm on the day of the game and he came rushing in and said, 'I'm changing it.' It was time for Plan C. Within thirty-three minutes of the first half we were 3–0 down and Stevie turned to me and deadpan said: 'This isn't working is it?'. Within seconds of the half-time whistle sounding he was scribbling away frantically on his notepad and in the dressing room he changed everything. We went out in the second half and demolished Ayr, scoring four goals in the space of eighteen minutes, going on to win 4–3. It was typical of Steve's speed of thought and tactical ability. He was forever thinking about the game and I don't think any manager ever switches off.

It worked well as a partnership. During matches I was the voice and Stevie would sit back quietly. He'd relay the occasional message through me to the players, otherwise the touchline was my domain. It was a far cry from my own time at Aberdeen when quite often we'd have Willie Miller, Roy Aitken and Drew Jarvie all having their say at the same time. More often than not you just wanted the three of them to stay quiet and let you get on with the game and leave you in peace. All you hear in that situation is noise and there simply can't be any clear direction when more than one person is involved.

Stevie and I avoided that overkill at all costs and it was the same in training. I'd take the warm-up while Steve was getting ready to do his tactical set-ups. He'd do a twenty-minute stint and then I'd take over and do another section of the session with them and we would keep rotating like that to make sure the boys were not hearing the same voice all of the time.

I think that was maybe half the problem with Alex Caldwell, who towards the end was finding it difficult to get through to some of the players. Barry Robson in particular made no secret of the fact that he didn't get on with Alex.

I found it incredibly difficult towards the end of Alex's time when certain players began to make it clear they would like me to get more involved. I didn't want him to think I was stepping on his toes and I certainly never set out to do that. Once it was done and the decision had been made for Alex to move on, it was a case of moving onwards and upwards and building a partnership between Stevie and me, on and off the park. With the pair of us working together we had a happy ship and that was a huge part of what we set out to achieve.

20

THE MANAGER, THE DEMONS
AND ME

The relationship between a manager and his assistant is never straightforward. In any working partnership there will always be good times and tough times, but the pairing between Steve Paterson and me was made an awful lot more complicated because it was a three-way marriage. There was him, me and the demons that plagued Steve.

Steve was forced to confront his problems with drink while he was in charge at Aberdeen. Everybody with a passing interest in Scottish football will remember the day that he went face-to-face with the media to admit he had an issue with binge drinking after he missed a match against Dundee at Pittodrie on the 'day after the night before'. It may have been a shocking admission for those looking in from the outside, but for me and others close to the man it came a few years too late.

I first noticed Steve's behaviour beginning to get erratic when we were at Caley Thistle. I can remember the game when it really became clear there was a big problem, on a Saturday afternoon in Greenock. We were due to play Clydebank at Cappielow and I'd arranged to spend a couple of days at Fort William before joining up with the team, who were spending the evening before the match at a hotel. John McAskill, the club doctor, lived in Fort

William, so I'd arranged to meet up with him in Greenock at the match and travel back together.

I got a call on the way down to the game on the Saturday morning to tell me to hurry to the hotel. The message was along the lines of 'Your man's in a hell of a state.'

It turned out that he had spent the night drinking with the doc and by the time the players came down for breakfast the pair of them were still in the corner of the room, John drinking whisky and Steve on the pints. You can imagine how much drink two Highlanders had got through in an all-night session.

We managed to get Steve to bed for a couple of hours – but by the time we got on the bus to go to Cappielow he was still steaming. He stood up to do his team talk in the dressing room and was obviously still half-cut. He wasn't making any sense at all and then all of sudden he turned to Denis Wyness and started taking the mickey out of him and having a joke, veering away from football and the game completely. It was like watching a drunk man at a wedding, standing on a table with people laughing at him. The thing was that Steve didn't mind that – he could laugh at himself and share the joke.

After the shambles in the dressing room, I took the boys out for the pre-match warm-up and then gathered them in a circle on the pitch for what was effectively a second team talk. I told them that it was obvious Stevie had problems, but if anyone owed the manager something it was them, that he had put his neck on the line for them and saved so many of their careers when it looked as though the only direction they were heading was backwards. I finished by telling them that football isn't about managers, it is about players. It was up to them to go out and do the business and the problems in the build-up were no excuse. They went out and to a man were absolutely magnificent, winning 3–0 to make a mockery of the problems in the build-up.

Steve was still pretty much well gone by the time we got on the bus to go back up the road. He'd leave his car at Ralia on the A9 and get off the coach there to drive across to Elgin and then home. That night he was in no state to drive, so I took the keys to the car and ferried him across to Moray.

That was an extreme case, but incidents like that became commonplace. Sunday was always his heavy drinking day and I'd often get a call from Graeme Bennett, the director of football, to come down and collect Stevie from the Caley club in Inverness after things had got out of control. He'd find a spare room to sleep in wherever he could. If he was on a big session at his golf club in Garmouth, I'd sometimes find him asleep in his car in a lay-by on the A96 when I was heading back up the road from Aberdeen. Frequently I'd get a call on Monday morning asking me to take training because he wasn't in a fit state to go to work.

It was a chaotic situation, but the problem was that Caley Thistle as a club were still learning what it meant to be a full-time professional side. They basically left Stevie to run the show and it was modelled in his mould, with a very blasé approach. If somebody was late for training it wasn't a problem; if somebody wanted a day off it wasn't a problem. Stevie was very much of the opinion that he needed his players most on a Saturday afternoon, so what went on in the week wasn't necessarily vital. It was a totally different approach from anything I'd experienced at any club I'd been at before, where being even a minute late was a heinous crime and daring to ask for a day off would be sneered at. On one occasion, at Swindon, young Fitzroy Simpson asked for the day off to go to his grandfather's funeral. The manager, Lou Macari, told him that there wasn't a lot Fitzroy could do for his grandad – he was dead. That was the end of that, it was back to training.

Steve's approach was the polar opposite and you can't argue with the results. Players would run through brick walls for the man because they knew he was on their side. He wasn't interested in battling against them and wanted to work with them. Those who did cross him wouldn't do it more than twice, though, he'd cut them out if they did. He didn't shout and scream, but he could be tough when he needed to be.

The drinking was the big fly in the ointment, but there was usually some sort of trigger to the worst episodes. The problems at the match down at Morton were sparked by a blazing row that Stevie had had with the chairman, Dougie McGilvray, over pension payments that hadn't been made. He had been promised quite a bit of money paid into a scheme but that hadn't happened and in the days leading up the game it came to a head, with the anger building up and building up.

By that stage Stevie had moved into my office, choosing to share with me rather than sit on his own. Part of that was for the company, but the other reason was that my office had a window – so he could have a sly cigarette.

Just a couple of days before we were due down in Cappielow we were sitting in the office and I could tell he was in a foul mood – something was bothering him. I could usually tell whether it was a good idea to talk to him or leave him to it. That day it was the latter. I was sitting doing my own thing when Stevie suddenly jumped up from his seat, threw open the window and shouted across the car park at Dougie McGilvray. He basically ordered the chairman inside and was baying for blood, I was convinced Stevie was ready to go for Dougie. I'd never seen him so mad in all my time with him, it was really vengeful stuff about the broken promises that the club had made. I could totally sympathise because in all my time as assistant manager I never had a proper contract – I was offered one plenty of times, but actually getting it on the table to be signed was a different matter altogether. I'd speak to Graeme Bennett, speak to the chairman and speak to the secretary Jim Falconer. It was always going to be ready tomorrow.

That was very much the way Caley Thistle was run in those days and it was obviously getting to Stevie. That day it all blew up and he left Dougie without a name. Eventually the chairman left and I managed to calm the manager down, but that weekend all the problems came to the fore again and he hit the bottle.

Stevie only ever got his contract situation resolved after Dundee United had come sniffing around on the back of their decision to sack Alex Smith in October 2002. We had our team at Inverness going well and were starting to attract attention. I got a call from Stevie to tell me he'd had a meeting with Eddie Thompson and had been offered the job at Tannadice, with a place for both of us if we wanted it. I wasn't on brilliant wages as assistant at Caley Thistle and the prospect of a big wage rise and a return to the Premier Division was an appealing one from my point of view. Stevie wasn't so sure though. Something about it didn't feel right to him and he took the decision to turn it down.

Then it all hit the fan. Eddie Thompson came out and said he'd never even met Stevie, let alone offered him the job. He was obviously terrified that whoever his second choice was (it turned out to be our old rival, Ian McCall) would take offence at being number two on the list of candidates.

Stevie was absolutely livid and felt his integrity was being questioned. He was never a publicity seeker, but that day he was straight onto the STV news to set the record straight about his meeting with Dundee United.

It was after that that Stevie went from working with no contract to signing a five-year deal. It went from the bizarre to the ridiculous, with that length of contract pretty much unheard of in management. I had a similar offer put to me, although I never did get round to signing it.

The contract worries brought on a lot of the dark moods that Stevie suffered from, although just as often those swings were caused by his gambling. Like every team up and down the land, we all liked to have a bet on the football, with the team bus stopping at Perth on the way south for away games and all of us piling into the bookie's to put a few quid on a coupon. Stevie was in a totally different league from any of us though.

He'd have four or five slips on the go every Saturday afternoon and they weren't the £5 or £10 lines the rest of us had on. Instead he'd bet hundreds of pounds at a time and he used Tommy Cummings, who doubled as groundsman and kitman then, as his first port of call for keeping track of how his bets were shaping up. During matches he'd have Tommy sitting with a radio earpiece keeping track of the scores. We'd be playing away in big games and Stevie would be busy getting score updates from some of the most obscure matches you could imagine, with Tommy shouting across the updates from Reading, Scunthorpe and any other outpost you can imagine. In between, Steve was relaying messages to the players through me on the touchline. Looking back, it was like a scene from a comedy sketch show.

Nobody at Caley Thistle could have been unaware of what was going on, but it was all forgiven because of the work we were doing with the team. Performances were exceptional, results were strong and the club was heading quickly in the right direction. There's no doubt in my mind that if we had stayed in Inverness, and managed to keep our squad together, we would have quickly been knocking on the door of the Premier League. Events overtook those plans though, with a rapid change in direction looming for us as 2002 drew to a close.

21

GOING HOME

It sounds like a cliché to say there was only one club I would have left Caley Thistle for, but that was genuinely the way I felt. Yes, the interest we had from Dundee United was tempting, but it was not the team that excited me. Aberdeen was the big chance I dreamed of as a coach and towards the end of 2002 it started to become clear that the opportunity was going to come quicker than Steve or I had anticipated.

While we were steadily working away in Inverness, down the A96 in Aberdeen the 2002/03 was turning into a disaster for the Dons and Ebbe Skovdahl. There had been some real hammerings in the league, with a 4–0 against Celtic at Pittodrie and then a 7–0 in the return game at Parkhead. The whispers started to grow about Ebbe's future and eventually he walked away, apparently feeling he didn't have the full backing of the board.

I still had good contacts at Pittodrie and towards the end of Ebbe's time in charge I began to get word that the writing was on the wall for the manager. At the same time I was being told that the chairman, Stewart Milne, was a big admirer of what Steve and I were doing at Inverness. I didn't tell Stevie any of that because I didn't want to give him any false hope – we'd spoken often enough in the past about Aberdeen being the perfect club for us.

When Ebbe left Pittodrie in December 2002, it quickly became clear that the steer I'd been given was accurate. The Dons board were keen on Stevie as the next manager. It quickly began to gather pace. Stewart and his board knew about some of the baggage Stevie carried with him in terms of his drinking, but I don't think any of them realised the extent of the problems. Whatever they knew didn't put them off and they set about putting together a package to make it happen, having to pay a decent compensation fee to Caley Thistle because of the lengthy contract Stevie had not long signed.

While Milne and his directors, headed by the chief executive Keith Wyness, set about enticing Steve to Aberdeen, there was a recruitment drive of a different kind being kicked off by their counterparts at the Caledonian Stadium.

On the day Steve went down to Aberdeen to speak to Stewart Milne, I was taken to one side by the Caley Thistle director of football Graeme Bennett in Inverness and offered the manager's job. They were convinced Stevie would take the job at Pittodrie and had moved quickly to get me to commit to take over from him. It was in no way black and white though. I knew a big part of the deal to take Stevie to Aberdeen was that I would be going with him. After the tough times they had gone through with Ebbe Skovdahl, taking someone who was already popular with the supporters would be a handy insurance policy and I could fill that role for them.

As far as Aberdeen were concerned I was part of the package and it was the same for Stevie. I don't think he would have gone to Pittodrie if I had said I wasn't making the move with him. So if I'd accepted the offer from Caley Thistle to become the manager at Inverness, I would have landed back at square one. Stevie would have decided not to go to Aberdeen and I would have ended exactly where I was, as assistant at Caley Thistle.

On paper I had a great opportunity in front of me to become a manager in my own right at a club that had a very solid team in place and was going places. In actual fact there wasn't a decision to make – I had to go with Stevie to Pittodrie. That was no hardship because it was the one job in Scotland that we both had our hearts set on.

We knew the north and north-east inside out and had a good handle on the market in that part of the country. We both had a passion for the club. In my case it was particularly strong, given the great times I'd had as a player there just a few years earlier. Geographically it was also perfect. I had loved living in the city and for Stevie it was close enough to his own patch in Moray to be comfortable. He has always been a home-bird and the prospect of straying too far from his friends and family in that corner of the world never really appealed. On top of all that, it was a move that trebled my salary and gave me financial security after the unpredictability at Caley Thistle.

I had a good idea that Aberdeen were waiting in the wings, and that was one of the reasons I never pushed Stevie to accept the Dundee United offer just a few weeks earlier. Tannadice would have been fine, but going back to Pittodrie was a dream move so early in my coaching career.

Despite my desire to move to the Dons, I spoke to Graeme Bennett and Kenny Cameron about the Caley Thistle manager's job and listened to what they had to say – but I think they realised that I was in a Catch-22 position. If I didn't go with Steve to Aberdeen, the manager's job they were offering me wouldn't exist. At the same time I think they had to be seen to be trying to persuade me to stay and take charge in my own right. I knew from what they were telling me that they had been getting good reports about the work I'd been doing as assistant manager and I would imagine they had sounded out a few of the senior players to canvas opinion. I knew the squad and the club, so I was well placed to keep things ticking over and try to maintain the progress we had been making.

By that time, Steve had been talking to Aberdeen for a couple of days and I had made brief contact to get a feel for the type of package I would be offered to go with him. I was upfront with Caley Thistle from start to finish and when they found out the wages I could earn at Pittodrie they were prepared to match it without hesitation. For a First Division side to make that type of commitment was a real indication of their determination, but it was all in vain. I had made my mind up that I was going – but still had to persuade Steve it was the right thing to do.

I needed no persuading, not least because I'd had a big vote of confidence from the Dons supporters in the days leading up to our move to Pittodrie. By coincidence I'd been booked to appear on the *Off the Ball* television programme, hosted by Tam Cowan. They were filming at the Music Hall in Aberdeen and while I was on the stage I was well aware that Steve was in talks at Pittodrie. It was a jokey type of show but I knew the question about the Dons job would be asked at some point during the night. I hoped I could avoid it, but sure enough it cropped up eventually. When it did come I played a straight bat and said I knew Steve was possibly heading for Pittodrie but had no idea whether I would be going too. The fact that the crowd had been singing my name in the hall that night was a gentle reminder that I'd be welcomed back with open arms.

Because I had that tie to the club it was an easy decision for me – but it wasn't my decision to make. On the night we finalised the move to Aberdeen I met up with Steve in the car park of the Eight Acres Hotel on the outskirts of Elgin. We were due to meet Keith Wyness, the Aberdeen chief executive, at the Linkwood Lodge Hotel on the other side of Elgin that evening, but Steve wanted time to talk things through with me.

We sat in the car for half an hour and in that time I managed to talk him into taking the job. He's one of life's deep thinkers and even then, with so much going on and so much to discuss, he wasn't giving too much away. What I could tell was that he wasn't sure about it and didn't think it was the right job for him. For one thing he told me that he didn't feel Keith had been open enough about the type of budget we would have to work with. But it was more than that. Stevie always went with his instinct and ninety-nine per cent of the time he was right. On this occasion his hunch was that he should turn down Aberdeen but he went against that, probably on my insistence. In the long run, in football terms at least, it did not pay off.

To this day, I feel terribly guilty about that. On the other hand, the experience at Aberdeen served to bring his problems to the fore. By exposing the issues with drink and gambling, I hope it helped him chase a few demons away. Had we stayed at Inverness I can only imagine Stevie would have slid even further into debt and further into drink.

Of course, what I didn't realise at the time was that he had a big motivation for taking the job, other than simply to keep me happy. Aberdeen were offering both of us a very hefty wage rise and with Steve's gambling habit he needed the money more than I knew. It's great to look back in hindsight and realise what was going on at the time, but I honestly didn't have any idea of the scale of his betting or the debt that he had accumulated as a result. The gambling was something that was easier to hide than the problems with drink. It is far easier to spot a drunk than it is a man who has just lost a fortune on the horses, although the dark moods would tend to give the game away.

I was more or less to blame for the decision to leave Inverness. Selfishly, I made it clear that I felt the Aberdeen job was the only one we had to go for. I didn't want to look back later in life and realise I'd blown the only chance I would ever have to go back to Pittodrie as part of the management team. I was determined to go for it.

I also felt that there were only so many jobs we could turn down before the phone stopped ringing. Steve would hark on about being overlooked by clubs but then when Dundee United came with an offer he didn't fancy it. Then it looked as though he would give Aberdeen the same answer and I felt that there may not be too many other opportunities if we went down that road again. It would have started to look as though no club could tempt us away from Inverness and that we were happy in that comfort zone.

From my point of view, the return to a good salary was welcome after a few years of lower wages with Caley Thistle. It was when I came to finalise my contract with the Dons that I realised how desperate they were to put Steve and me in place. The first offer I had from Keith Wyness was turned down flat. He asked me to go back with a figure that I felt was reasonable and to my total amazement he said yes on the spot. In fact, I'd plucked a figure out that I felt was far higher than the club would agree to, in the hope of meeting somewhere in the middle. The fact that Keith accepted it without trying to haggle suggested he needed to return from Elgin that night with both of our signatures on contracts to keep Stewart Milne pacified. The truth of the matter is that I would have agreed to whatever had been on the table to get back to Aberdeen. Even if he had said that the first offer was the final offer I would have taken the job.

I found Keith Wyness a pleasure to work with. I know not everyone in football appreciated his style or his methods but from start to finish I felt he was the ideal chief executive. From those early negotiations, he was honest and straightforward to deal with and once we were in place at Pittodrie his door was always open. I would often sit down and talk things through with Keith and I was impressed by his football knowledge and views on the game. You don't get to work at the top of the English game in any capacity if you are not a good operator and the fact that Keith went on to play a major role with Everton suggests his abilities were appreciated further afield. I certainly wouldn't bet against seeing him back in Scottish football in a prominent role and it was no surprise to see him mentioned for the chief executive's position at the SFA when Gordon Smith resigned in 2010.

By the end of the night of negotiations in Elgin, we had the fine details thrashed out and both of us signed the paperwork, faxing it through from a house in Elgin to finalise everything. I think there was relief all round – not least on the club's side. They had the combination they had wanted from the minute Ebbe Skovdahl had walked away.

I was part of the package as far as Aberdeen were concerned and I suppose it was a bit of a coup to get me back, given that our stock was pretty high then. The next day we went back to Inverness to pack up our gear from the stadium and say our goodbyes. I was excited, having moved around often enough to get used to it, but for Stevie it was a big wrench. He'd built up a side at Caley Thistle and had strong bonds with a lot of the players he was leaving behind. Once it was done it was done. As soon as we pitched up in Aberdeen the anticipation began to kick in.

22

INTO THE RED

So much energy had been put into making the move from Caley Thistle to Aberdeen a reality that we hadn't had too much time to consider the job that was facing us at Pittodrie. The reality hit home pretty quickly and we knew from our first day at the club that we had a massive task if we were to rebuild the team in the way we and the board wanted to.

The remit on paper was simple: arrest the decline in results, ship out the expensive imported players and introduce a new crop of predominantly Scottish talent. The emphasis was on bringing through as many youngsters as we could, while all the time cutting the wage bill to try and address the financial problems that had arisen from some of the wild spending in the years before our arrival.

It was a tall order, but it didn't frighten us. What did scare me was what we found when we got our hands on the squad we had to work with. The first training session was very upbeat. We played three small-sided games in short bursts and you could see in an instant the players who had the heart for it. There were some who were absolutely flying, obviously busting a gut to impress, and others who clearly didn't give a damn.

After training we had our first team talk. Steve said a few words and I said my piece too. While the manager was talking, my eye was drawn to Roberto Bisconti, the Belgian midfielder who had earned rave reviews after arriving the previous season. By the time we got our hands on him, it looked as though his motivation had fallen through the floor. All through Steve's team talk he sat slouched in the corner with his arms folded, shaking his head at just about every point that was being made. He was a complete and utter disgrace. The meeting finished and I told Steve what I'd seen. He said: 'Don't worry, Duncan. I clocked him. He'll be the first out the door.'

One by one we had to weed out the characters who had dragged the place down and killed the family spirit that I remembered from my time as a player. The canteen used to be a buzzing, happy place to be. Now it was so quiet you could hear a pin drop, with different cliques sitting in silence in all four corners. It was horrible and in an instant we knew the problems ran far deeper than we had anticipated.

There were far too many foreign players on the books when we came to it. That is not me being narrow-minded, more an observation about the balance of the squad. There's no doubt there are players you have to look far and wide for to add an extra something to any squad – but the key is to blend those imported men in with a core of guys who have a real feel for the country and more importantly the club. The group we were landed with just didn't have that affinity with Aberdeen, or even Scottish football. Most of them looked as though they weren't interested.

It was a major exercise to put that right and fortunately there was scope to bring in extra help. What had been a two-man team became a trio when Steve appointed Oshor Williams as coach. The two of them went right the way back to their time together as apprentices at Manchester United, but I had only met Oshor once, when he came along to watch Caley Thistle. I guess the two of them had a pact to take one another along if either of them got a big job.

Myself, Stevie and Oshor Williams were put up in a flat in Mannofield and there was no time to waste after inheriting a team that was in freefall. I got to know Oshor well in the months ahead and I was very impressed with what I found. Like me, he was prepared to work 24/7 to make a go of the opportunity we had with Aberdeen. The two of us racked up thousands of miles watching opposition teams and scouting for players during the time we had at the club. From the start I tried to explain to Steve that we couldn't afford to have as much as a day off if it was going to work for us, that we didn't have time to waste. I don't think he shared my sense of urgency.

Oshor had come from a role with the PFA in England rather than a traditional club background and I think that worked against him. Bad professionals will look at a coach in terms of what they have done and who they know, not what they know. Bad professionals blame a coach for their own shortcomings and then go to another club and blame a different coach. Eventually you would think these players would realise that the deficiencies were on their side.

Good professionals will listen and recognise a good coach when they are working with one. Oshor was one who fell into that category and one of those who deserved respect. The more I spoke to him, the more I realised how intelligent he is when it comes to football. It is no surprise that he has settled back into a very good job with the PFA's education arm.

We also brought Neale Cooper back to the club, following his spell in charge at Forfar Athletic. I'd seen Neale working with the youth teams at Pittodrie during my time as a player and was always impressed. He pushed the kids hard because he wanted them to be the best they could be. I was surprised he had ever been allowed to leave in the first place, when Ebbe Skovdahl deemed him surplus to requirements. It's fitting that Neale has remained on the staff through the various changes in management since Steve and I took him back early in 2003.

Jim Leighton was the only coach we inherited from the previous regime and his expertise was valuable. I really felt for him when he was discarded by Mark McGhee. He didn't deserve that after the service he gave to the club over three decades in various forms.

Mind you, Jim is long enough in the tooth to know how the game works and has displaced a few goalkeepers in his time. I remember when he was brought back to Pittodrie in 1997 as a player, with the rumours flying about the city in the weeks leading up to the move. We were playing Partick Thistle down at Firhill when Nicky Walker, who was the recognised No.1 at that stage, started shouting up at the stand. From the other end of the pitch I could hear him bawling, 'I can see you Jim, I can see you.' Sure enough, there was Mr Leighton at the back of the stand. He was obviously along for a little look before signing on the dotted line.

He came in and took the shirt off Nicky's back and was still there when I returned five years later. Jim did a sterling job for us, although to be fair he had some excellent goalkeepers to work with at that time. Peter Kjaer and David Preece were the two vying for a starting place and both were more than capable. Which is more than can be said for some of the players we were landed with at Pittodrie.

As I mentioned, Roberto Bisconti was one we had to get shot of. It turned out he had problems off the field as well as on it. He had rented a house and left the place in a terrible state, with the car he was using in similar condition. I didn't feel as though he had any respect for us, yet he was raking in £4,500 a week.

Eric Delemeaux was another who was earning money that we found very difficult to justify on the basis of his performances in training and in matches. I'm sure he had ability but he didn't have the stomach for it. We'd send the players out to do a few circuits of the training ground and he could barely manage a couple of times round before he fell two laps behind the rest of them. Whether he wasn't physically able to do it or just didn't fancy it, we'll never know.

Leon Mike would be trailing behind with Eric in the fitness work. He was a lovely big guy who always had a big smile on his face, but I never believed he had what it took to be a successful Aberdeen striker. We kept him on for a period but it just wasn't working, no matter how hard we tried to work him, and he disappeared out of football after returning back home to England.

There were others who were never going to fit in with what we wanted to do. The Italian defender, Patrizio Billio, was a cracking character, a really nice guy, but as a player he wasn't the answer. We needed a dominant type of player to slot in alongside Zander Diamond, who was just about to break through, and that wasn't Billio.

Ben Thornley was one who I was sure had something to give, but he'd had injury problems that really kept him on the fringes. Eventually he was moved on to make room in the squad.

Peter Kjaer, a great goalkeeper with real presence and experience, was another who fell by the wayside. Ebbe Skovdahl would take David Preece into the side for the occasional cup tie or game when Peter was away on international duty with Denmark and then slot the big Scandinavian back into the team as soon as he was available. That was never going to happen under Steve and me. When David came in and did well, he kept his place. The team was picked on merit. Peter didn't take too kindly to that and it got to the stage where it was time for him to move on for a fresh challenge.

David did really well for us. Having been nothing more than a back-up player under the previous manager, he grabbed the chance with both hands. If a player does well then he deserves to keep his place, no matter who is waiting in the wings. The added bonus was that he also saved us another big wage by stepping up to the plate and allowing us to let Peter leave.

All in all, we worked out we shaved more than £7,000 off the weekly wage bill during our eighteen months in charge. That was part of the remit Steve had been given by Stewart Milne, who wanted a shift towards a team of Scottish players with potential. The chairman didn't want that at any cost, though, and we were expected to overhaul the squad while at the same time working with a vastly reduced budget.

To do that we turned to the First Division, a market we knew inside out, as well as Aberdeen's own youth set-up. The likes of Chris Clark, Russell Anderson, Phil McGuire and Kevin McNaughton were already established, but there were others ready to be pushed forward. Zander Diamond was still raw and rough around the edges but we could see he was ready to be given a chance, certainly better than the likes of Billio and some of the others we had inherited. We also blooded Richard Foster amongst others.

They needed the support of experienced professionals alongside them and we struck gold when we landed Steve Tosh from Falkirk. He was everything an Aberdeen player should be, with a real steel and determination. Within a week of arriving, Tosh was fighting with others in the dressing room because he couldn't stand the attitudes of some of them. He had that fighting spirit but could also play and quickly won over the supporters.

Jamie McQuilken was a player who should have had the same impact but never did. We had watched him terrorise teams in the First Division, marauding up and down the wing, but when he came to Aberdeen from Falkirk he just seemed to take fright. I don't know if it was the pressure of playing for a big club or if it was living away from his family. Whatever it was, Jamie just crumbled. He never really managed to rebuild his career after a horrible time with Aberdeen and certainly never played to the standards that we knew he was capable of.

Markus Heikkinen was a different story altogether. We picked up Markus on a free transfer after he had fallen out of contract at Helsinki and landed up on trial with us during pre-season in 2003. He was one of the few players we took on trial from the hundreds we were offered. After one game in Bradford during that summer period we decided to sign him. The lists of players we got at Aberdeen were ten times as long as the ones we got at Caley Thistle, with agents obviously aware there was a bit more gold to be had at Pittodrie than there was in Inverness. For every 100 names, there was one worth taking a closer look at. Markus, who had been on loan at Portsmouth before arriving in Scotland with us, proved to be a real gem of a find.

David Zdrilic was one who looked as though he would fall into the same category but never managed to find the consistency of performance suggested by some of his early displays. David was a great finisher and loved to stay back after training and spend forty minutes with me and a goalkeeper doing shooting practice. Unfortunately that was all he wanted to do – he would question why we had to do anything else in training. Eventually I had to tell him we'd do it because I was the coach and he was a player. He had an opinion about everything and eventually it would wear you down. David scored some spectacular and important goals – a prime example was his strike in the famous win we had down at Celtic in 2003.

Leigh Hinds, another of the forwards we recruited, didn't have the same success. I was disappointed it didn't work out for Leigh because there was no question that he had the ability. Against Caley Thistle he had always been a real nuisance when he played for Clyde. What probably counted against him was he had a lethargic look about him, particularly in training. In the end I think that was what cost him his place at Aberdeen, because Jimmy Calderwood took one look at him and thought he was lazy. In fact, when Leigh moved from training into games he was a different animal and was a real handful.

Paul Sheerin was typical of the type of player we had to go looking for. Paul had wonderful ability and was an individual we knew as a player and as a character. He came in for a small fee and on a wage that was a quarter of the amount the high-earning overseas players were draining from the club. He produced a good return in terms of goals and performances, and some Dons supporters shouted for him to be involved in the Scotland set-up after his good start with the club.

We would love to have been able to add Barry Robson to that mix too. Money was the stumbling block, even though we really pushed the boat out to make Barry a good offer to come back to his home patch in the north-east. We knew the potential he had and the type of heights he could scale if he had the right platform to play on. When we found out that Barry was about to sign for Dundee United we tried to hijack the deal but we couldn't pull it off. As United found out, it was a very solid investment and if the money could have been found to take him to Pittodrie the directors would have seen a very healthy return.

Dean Windass on the other hand was a player we could have signed but chose not to. When we went to England for pre-season we faced up to Deano's Bradford side and I told Steve and Oshor to watch what he would do to Russell Anderson and Phil McGuire. I told them that they would just bounce off Dean and sure enough they did, quite literally. He was getting the ball played up to his feet and just shielded it from our two young defenders, tensing up his body and knocking the pair of them to the ground as though they were made of paper. After the game Dean was pleading with me to take him back to Aberdeen, offering to take a big pay cut to make it happen. As much as I would have liked to have had him in the team at that point, it simply wouldn't have worked. I told him there was no way I could shout him down in matches or in training and then go out for a beer with him like we did in the good old days when we were team-mates. It would have been a different relationship and neither of us would have been comfortable in that situation.

Instead of going back to old favourites, we had to look for new players to bring into the club or promote through the ranks. We didn't take too many in on trial and the ones we did were easy to make a judgement on. I've always said it takes me five minutes to recognise a football player. Everything from the way a player dresses and carries himself on the park to the way he addresses the ball and strikes it can be seen within seconds of hitting the training ground.

Steve operated in a similar sort of way and I remember him taking one look at Scott Michie and telling me he would never be a top-level striker. I asked him why and Steve turned to me and said: 'Can you see any other player with their sleeves pulled over their hands?' Right enough, Scott was moaning about the cold and that attitude was a telltale sign. Obviously he had talent to get to the fringes of the first team, but to make it to the very top you need that extra something and it is easy to tell which individuals have that desire and which ones don't.

Chris Clark was clearly a great young player who had that drive to succeed – but we couldn't figure out his best position. Was it wide on the left, wide on the right or through the middle? All I did know was that he couldn't finish for love nor money. He had brilliant skills on the ball until you put him in front of goal and then it all fell to pieces.

Kevin McNaughton was a similar age and an absolute joy to work with. He would listen and take on board everything he was told, a model professional and exemplary young player.

While we were fortunate to have success with many of the new recruits, there were misses as well as the hits. Michael Bird, a young striker released by Bolton, was one of Oshor's finds and he hardly set the heather alight. He was a tall lad and potentially had the physical attributes to be a useful striker – but everything was somebody else's fault, whether in a game or in training. His head wasn't in the right place, although being a young boy many miles from home probably didn't help.

When you list the players who came and went in the space of a single summer in 2003 it is quite staggering. Some people might argue it was too much too soon – but when you consider the state of the squad when we arrived, the changes really couldn't come quickly enough.

After arriving in December 2002 we enjoyed a revival in the second half of the season and any fears that we would be stuck in a relegation fight were quickly dismissed when we started putting points on the board. In the last ten games of the Premier League season we lost only twice and that helped us stabilise the club to finish in eighth place. It wasn't spectacular, but we were moving in the right direction and ended up with more points than fifth-placed Dunfermline because of the daft split in the SPL.

We had started the season with Caley Thistle aiming for promotion and finished it with a successful climb away from the relegation zone with Aberdeen. In between there had been drama off the pitch that nobody could have predicted, and as we headed into the summer of 2003 everyone was hoping for a fresh start in more ways than one.

23

THE BIG CRASH

I always wanted to manage Aberdeen. What I hadn't anticipated was the bizarre way that opportunity would present itself. The date I got my chance to take charge of the Dons was 15 March 2003, but I would gladly give up that little claim to fame to be able to turn back the clock and start that day all over again.

That was the day on which Steve Paterson went absent without leave, failing to report for duty for the home game against Dundee in the SPL, after his well-publicised drinking binge the night before. As it happened, I emerged from my brief tenure with an unbeaten record, drawing 3–3 on the day, but it has to rank as the worst and most fraught day of my professional life.

Within days, all of the dirty washing had been aired in public as Steve had his confessional in front of the press. What has never been explained before is the frantic efforts the rest of us were making behind the scenes to try and limit the damage to both the club and Stevie's own career. Given we were very much a partnership, I was also fighting for my own future in what was a horrendous period for everyone caught up in it.

The problems began to build two days before we were due to play Dundee, when Steve had one of his serious drinking sessions on the Thursday night. The first I knew of that was when he rolled into work on the Friday morning looking as though he was still buzzing from the night before, with his hair all ruffled and generally looking the worse for wear.

We got through training as normal but that night we had a club dinner at the Beach Ballroom as part of the centenary celebrations. The coaching staff were expected to be there, along with everyone else on the payroll at Pittodrie, and I knew that it wouldn't take too many glasses of wine to top Steve up after the amount he'd obviously had the night before.

The unfortunate thing was that I was on a different table, so had no idea what state he was in as the night wore on. To be fair, it would probably have ended without incident if we hadn't been invited to head into town with the rest of the club staff at the end of the function. I didn't think it was a wise idea but he didn't need to be asked twice and I ended up tagging along to try and keep him out of mischief.

The group headed for Paramount in the city centre, a bar where I never felt comfortable. It's the type of place footballers are supposed to love, full of £1,000 suits and people wanting to be seen. There are hundreds of clubs and bars like it up and down the country that have the football fraternity flocking to their doors, but places like that have never been for me. I was far more comfortable at less pretentious places and after we'd had a drink with everyone I suggested to Steve that we should slip away quietly before the party got into full swing. I said I'd take him across the road to O'Donoghues for a pint of Guinness then get him home, but it fell on deaf ears.

When Stevie's had a drink he becomes everyone's best friend and he was enjoying having a laugh and joke with the staff, not least because every new person he spoke to came with a drink for him in their hand. Eventually I gave up trying to talk sense into him and left him to it. I didn't storm out or anything like that, but not for the first time I was disappointed with him and he knew I was fed up.

I later found out that while I was tucked up in bed, the manager had been painting the town red until the early hours. I must have left him at around midnight to go home and get a decent night's sleep before the Dundee game. He had stayed out drinking until chucking out time and then followed our physio John Sharp home and ended up sinking another bottle of wine at John's house, before eventually making it home to the flat where he was staying at Mannofield. It was the place that Oshor and I had shared with him after initially taking the job, but by then my family had moved down from Inverness and we had settled into our own place in Rosemount. Oshor, whose wife and two kids had moved up from England, was staying in Balmedie.

That left Stevie on his own and that turned out to be bad news. I was up bright and early and down at Pittodrie by 11.45am. That was the time when Oshor and I would usually meet up at the ground on the day of a home game to run through set pieces and other preparations in the office. Oshor wasn't at the Dundee game, having been granted leave because a good friend of his and Stevie's had gone through the horror of his son committing suicide. That was one of the reasons Steve cited for his heavy drinking around that time.

Instead, it was myself and Neale Cooper who were laying out the plans, and eventually we began to worry as the minutes ticked by and there was still no sign of the boss. David Johnston put his head round the door as he normally did on a match day to see if there was anything he could do for us, but I decided not to let on that I was beginning to fear we had a problem.

By 12.30pm there was still no word and by then I'd tried his mobile and the phone at the flat without any joy. My heart was thumping, going ten to the dozen, and I was genuinely worried about Steve. It was nothing to do with the fact that we had a match looming at that point; it was more genuine concern that he could be lying in a heap somewhere in real trouble.

I got hold of John Sharp and he told me he'd seen Stevie home at 2.30am. He didn't tell me at that point that he'd treated him to another bottle of wine just before, but I don't blame him for what happened. John was never a shrinking violet when it came to having a good night out – but he knew the difference between being professional and being stupid. He's the best physio I've ever worked with and I don't think you could accuse him of leading Stevie astray that night. He didn't need any encourage-ment when there was drink involved and always wanted to be the last man standing.

From speaking to John, I at least knew that Steve had made it back to the flat. My father-in-law was up visiting that weekend and the two of us jumped in the car and sped round to Mannofield. I was standing on the doorstep buzzing the intercom. When I got no response I tried every button on the panel to try and raise somebody to let me in the main entrance. I couldn't get any answer and even tried throwing stones at the windows. Still there was no sign of life.

Time was getting on and I had no option but to get back through the traffic and back to Pittodrie, by which point it was around about 1.30pm and the game was fast approaching.

By then Keith Wyness had obviously sussed that something was amiss and came looking for answers. As much as I'd always tried to protect Stevie in the past, this time it was impossible. Keith took me aside and said: 'It's a simple question: where the hell is he?'

I said: 'I've got a simple answer: I've got no idea.' I knew John had taken him home, but with no reply on the phone or at the flat he could have been anywhere. The worry was that he might have gone out looking to carry on the party.

In a sense it was a relief to be able to be honest with Keith. For too long I'd covered up for Stevie; looked good people in the eye and lied to them to try and keep him out of trouble.

Those people must have known I was lying and I absolutely hated it. I hated myself for doing it, but at times felt like I didn't have a choice.

Now it had gone past the stage of being able to pull the wool over anyone's eyes. Keith and the rest of the board must have known they were taking a risk by employing Steve but they possibly underestimated just how big that was. He'd been late before for matches at Caley Thistle, but there he had directors who were willing to put up with it. At Aberdeen Football Club there was never going to be the same tolerance because there are shareholders and people the manager is accountable to.

After talking things through briefly, Keith decided to give Stevie another fifteen or twenty minutes. There was still no sign and, with just an hour to go before kick-off, he asked me to take the team for the day.

I had no problem with that. Everything was already in place in terms of the team selection and tactics, so it was really a case of thinking on my feet and coming up with a team talk to rally the troops. Keith and I agreed we should tell the players that Steve had been held up, in the forlorn hope that he'd come breezing through the door before 3pm.

I stood in the dressing room and relayed that message, but I would imagine a good few of the squad had figured out the real story. By then the reports of the night before would have been flying around the staff and it wouldn't take long for the stories to reach the players.

I basically reverted to the team talk that I'd used against Clydebank years earlier, when Stevie was there in body but not in mind. This time it was the Aberdeen players I was addressing, not the Caley Thistle squad, but the message was the same: whether there's a manager on the touchline or not doesn't matter one bit if each and every one of the eleven men on the park does his own job. If players can do that, a manager becomes an irrelevance.

The game itself was as bizarre as the circumstances it was played in. We were 2–0 down by half-time, with Steve Lovell and Fabian Caballero scoring early on. I remember walking up the touchline with Neale Cooper going in for the interval and saying to him that we had to make changes. We did that, tinkered with one or two things in terms of shape but not personnel, and it had the desired effect. As I had told the players at half-time, we weren't good enough to come back from three goals behind but if we got back in the game with a goal to make it 2–1 then it was game on. We battled back level with a double from Paul Sheerin after the break and with ten minutes left on the clock a Phil McGuire goal put us ahead. Within seconds Lee Wilkie had equalised. It was typical of our luck that day.

I've read quotations from Jimmy Calderwood and Mark McGhee, talking about the long walk from the dugout in front of the Main Stand to the tunnel in the corner beside the Richard Donald Stand and that is something I can sympathise with entirely. That afternoon it was the longest thirty seconds of my life. There were no boos or jeers, but there was a really strange atmosphere. The supporters knew there was something going on and they were looking for answers.

I hurried down the side of the pitch and into the dressing room. I thanked the players for their efforts, particularly in coming back from two goals down when other teams could have crumbled. I told them that I wasn't going to lie to them, that something had gone awry with the manager and that everything would be explained on Monday when we sat down and talked through the events of that weekend.

The next thing I had to do was face the press, but first I had to talk to the chief executive and find out how he wanted me to approach it. It was then that Keith told me he'd spoken to Steve and that the party line was that he had been suffering from stomach cramps and hadn't been well enough to attend the match.

I walked into the press room hoping I'd be able to avoid the question altogether – but naturally enough it was the first thing I was asked. I explained the situation as Keith had relayed it to me from his conversation with the manager, telling the reporters that he had called in sick but left instructions for the game. More lies.

Once the crowds had cleared I went home, dropped off my father-in-law, then headed round to Steve's flat. He let me in and what I saw shocked me. He looked far worse than I'd ever seen him before – and I'd seen him in some states in the past. Given this was nearly eighteen hours after he'd stopped drinking and landed in his bed, it was a worrying state of affairs. The first thing he did was ask me the score, so obviously he'd been too frightened to turn on the television and see what was being said about the whole debacle of a day.

I spent a good couple of hours with him and he had a lot to get off his chest. He was also trying to piece together the night before and said he thought he'd been at John Sharp's house. I was able to tell him he had, but it was an indication of just how far gone he must have been. It turned out that he'd collapsed into bed at 3am and conked out for nearly twelve hours. He woke up at 2.45pm, took one look at the clock and went back to sleep. I can't begin to imagine what was going on in his head but he must have just given up. He knew he was about to miss the game and didn't care.

We sat with a cup of tea and talked things over. By then he'd been told to report to Stewart Milne's house for a meeting at noon the following day. What I heard next alarmed me – Steve was planning to head to his mother's house in Moray to spend the night. The Garmouth Hotel on his home patch had been his undoing throughout his life. It was a dangerous place for him to go because it usually led to a big drinking session with his mates there. I was terrified about what was about to happen but

I didn't even bother warning him. It felt like we were too far down the road to self-destruction to try and turn back.

I went home and told my wife to prepare for the worst, that I didn't think there was any way Steve was coming back from this one. I didn't want to scare Michele but I wanted to warn her about what I was sure was going to happen, because the only outcome I could see from the meeting between the manager and the chairman was his dismissal. If he was sacked then obviously myself and Oshor would be axed with him. Even though we had uprooted the family from Inverness and taken the kids out of school to make the move back to Aberdeen, Michele was very pragmatic about the situation. Knowing I had her support was important to me. As long as she was on my side I was prepared for whatever happened next.

I woke up on the Sunday morning with a really strange mindset. Just as I'd been waiting by the phone when it first became clear that Aberdeen wanted to recruit the pair of us, now I was sitting hanging on for a call to tell me that I'd lost the job that meant so much to me.

In fact, when the phone rang it was Steve's number that popped up on the screen and it was before the meeting had even taken place. I was worried about what state he'd be in but I was relieved to hear that he sounded fresh and was thinking clearly. He told me he hadn't touched a drop of drink on the Saturday night and just needed to get back to explain things to his mum and get his head together.

I pottered around the house for a few hours until the meeting broke up and Steve called me back. What I wasn't expecting was the news that we all had jobs to go back to on Monday. He said: 'The first thing to say is I've not been sacked.' That shocked me.

I was expecting to find out he had been hit by a heavy fine but instead it had turned on its head. Steve had agreed to go public about his drink problem and in return the club had agreed to support him as he tried to overcome it. Really they had little choice. Because alcoholism is classed as a disease, there was no way the club could have sacked Steve after he had come clean about the situation. They had to be seen to be doing the right thing and helping him through it. His side of the bargain involved attending counselling sessions and I believe he did that. Against all the odds it looked as though the storm had been weathered and it was back to business as usual.

24

LIVING ON BORROWED TIME

The aftermath of the Dundee debacle was a surreal period for all of us wrapped up in the whole sorry mess. I had prepared for the worst and expected to be sacked along with Steve and Oshor Williams. When it became clear that the manager had been given a reprieve, I still felt in my heart of hearts that the clock was ticking. In fact, the clock had ticked as far as I was concerned – I was certain we were a sacking waiting to happen.

Perhaps it would have been better for everyone if there had been a clean break at that point, rather than having the uncertainty hanging over us for more than a year after that terrible day. We all did our best to put it behind us and concentrate on the job in hand, but it was difficult not to feel as though we were dead men walking.

The first stage of the apparent redemption was for Stevie to face the nation's media and reveal Scottish football's worst kept secret: he was battling a drink problem. The image of him sitting in that press conference, side by side with Keith Wyness, was an emotive one. He looked like a little boy lost. I can't begin to imagine what he was going through that day, when he had to lay his soul bare in front of a room packed with reporters, camera crews and radio microphones. It was a big thing for him to do but a necessary evil if he wanted to keep his job.

The two of us had actually been given media training when

we were appointed by Aberdeen. The directors had brought in a public relations company to brief us on the way we should approach interviews and to outline the image we should be trying to portray. Everything from body language to tone of voice was covered and the training also included a role-play session in front of television cameras in which Steve had to field a series of mock questions.

Ironically the scenario we were given to deal with was a about a fictitious incident involving one of our players in a nightclub, in which he had been arrested. I came up with the textbook answer, saying that we would have to wait for police reports and to speak to the player before releasing a statement. Then the mock interviewer cut in to say it was the second incident that particular player had been involved in within a week. My response was to swear and say the bugger would be kicked out the door before his feet could touch the ground. Stevie was in the corner killing himself laughing and so was Stewart Milne, who also took part in the media training. My response wasn't quite the one you'd find in the media manual, but I guess it proved the point about the type of pressure you can be under when it comes to press conferences.

The whole media training exercise was planned with the best of intentions. Stewart could see how uncomfortable Steve was under the media spotlight and wanted to help him. He wanted to teach him how to carry himself in front of the press and to put on a positive performance in front of the cameras. What he couldn't have predicted were the circumstances in which Stevie would face his biggest media test. I can't imagine too many of the golden rules of dealing with the press were running through his mind as he sat there explaining why he had missed the Dundee game and giving an account of how serious his drinking problems were.

He maintained that it was binge drinking rather than alcoholism that was his downfall and promised that he would be able to control it with the right help and support. True enough, Steve did not touch a drop to drink for three months after his summit meeting with Stewart Milne and that press conference to confront the issue.

Although he had gone those twelve weeks without a dram, I didn't expect for a minute that he had drunk his last drink. I had worked with him long enough to be certain there was no way on earth he would be able to stay dry and had conversations with Oshor about it. He knew Steve as well as anyone and assured me the drinking was under control. He tried to reassure me that everything was back on the straight and narrow. I only wish I could have shared his optimism.

Sure enough, before too long the little warning signs began to flash up. The mood swings that I'd first begun to take notice of at Caley Thistle began to resurface and the arrival times in the morning become a bit more erratic, another factor that had reared its head at Inverness and usually pointed to a good drinking session the night before. There were times we'd be preparing to start training at 10am and Stevie would bowl in with ten minutes to spare, which was not the level of professionalism you need at a club the size of Aberdeen, or the right image to portray to the players you're trying to preach discipline to.

In saying that, there were no major relapses – or certainly nothing as catastrophic as the day of the Dundee game. Missing that match was as bad as it ever got for Stevie, either at Inverness or Pittodrie, and I suppose with that as a benchmark there was never likely to be anything as bad.

What there was during the period between the problems being made public and the day we eventually left the club was a constant worry that today would be the day that it collapsed around us again. Working under that sort of strain is no good for anyone.

The difficulty for me was that I didn't socialise with Steve, so I was totally in the dark about what he was up to away from the club. That could be seen as either a blessing or a curse. On match days or after training we'd spend an hour or so chewing the fat and then all go our separate ways. I'd head home to Westhill, where we eventually moved to, and Oshor would shoot off up the road to Balmedie. Stevie would go back to his home patch in Moray and back into the bosom of his old drinking buddies. That's not a criticism of the company he kept – I grew up in the same sort of village environment as he did and I know fine well that if I'd been living near Caol I would have whiled away the hours with my old pals in the pub, just like he did.

After the initial hullabaloo had died down, Stevie was back being left to his own devices and the choice was his. He could stay on the wagon, get his head down and try to salvage the situation or slip back into old habits. Initially he did knuckle down, but circumstances the following season gave him a good excuse to revert to the bad ways. We were working with our hands tied behind our back because of budget cuts and, perhaps not surprisingly, the results were not as we would have hoped. The strain began to build and take its toll on Steve, which was hardly ideal for somebody in such a fragile state of mind.

To compound the pressures at work, he still had to contend with the media interest. By admitting he was addressing a drink problem, he had laid himself open to a very public examination. It felt as though everything he said or did was being analysed and people were ready to pounce on the slightest hint that things weren't right with his personal circumstances. He only got caught off-guard a couple of times, mainly because he put the shutters up and did his best to limit his contact with the press and supporters as much as he could. But speculation about his position began to mount when the team's form took a turn for the worse.

The rumours also began to spring up that Willie Miller was being lined up to come back to the club in some capacity. We knew there was rarely any smoke without fire and Steve told me then and there that if Willie came in he knew he would be packing his bags.

Stevie was the antithesis of everything Willie had been as a manager. Whereas Willie's sessions were planned to the letter, Steve flew by the seat of his pants. There was one Monday during that final season when I booked the day off after a wedding in Fort William at the weekend and Oshor was also given time off to visit family in England. Steve was fine with that and said he'd take training. It wasn't until three weeks later that I discovered he had called Steve Tosh on the morning to ask him to take training. It was incredible, but still there was no rebuke from high office, even though they must have been aware of the things that were going on.

There were plenty of scouting trips to England that I know fine well ended in a pub rather than at a football stadium. He'd duck away, claiming to watch games when he was really going south to hook up with old friends for a good session.

I suppose I could have gone to Keith Wyness and told him about my concerns, but that wasn't my place. It's the old unwritten rule in football that loyalty is a given and that what happens in the dressing room or on the training field stays there. It would have been easy to confide in Keith, who I got on with very well, but I never once discussed Steve's situation with him or the chairman. Maybe I should have stepped in and offered to take over for a period, to allow Stevie to get away from it all and get his head together – but that was never discussed and wasn't something I would have been comfortable suggesting. Instead I did what I could to hold things together and to try and make sure the players were not distracted, as hard as that was to do.

There were so many people around who knew what was going on, from the physios in the treatment room to the players and the office staff, that to my mind it was impossible that the chiefs did not know what was happening. It was their business to know.

To their credit, neither Stewart Milne nor Keith Wyness ever put me in the difficult position of having to be Steve's keeper. Not once did they come to me and ask me about his movements or try and get me to report back to them. I think they knew anyway that, whatever had happened, our working relationship would be totally compromised if there was even the slightest suspicion that I was going behind Steve's back in that manner.

In any case, they didn't need me doing their detective work for them. There are no secrets at a football club and Aberdeen is no different. Davie Johnston, the general manager, would call into our offices in the morning with his clipboard to check if there was anything we needed. He'd find Oshor and me at our desks at 9am but, in that final season, there was rarely, if ever, any sign of the manager. My phone would ring while Davie was in the room, with Steve on the other end telling me to say he was ten minutes away. I knew that ten minutes away probably meant he was passing through Huntly and was still forty-five minutes away from the ground. The late starts were as much down to his appalling timekeeping as anything else.

It was totally the opposite of my own attitude. I'd had the importance of punctuality drummed into me when I was growing up and again during my playing days, not least at Aberdeen, when so much play was made of representing the club in the right manner.

Davie was very much of the same mindset and I knew fine well that with every late arrival he would be going straight upstairs to report to Keith Wyness. That's no criticism of Davie, who would not have been doing his job if he hadn't been keeping a close watch on everything that was going on in the football department. That was his remit after all.

After the Dundee incident, I never lied to cover for Steve or tried to hide anything from the club – it would have been impossible to do that even if I'd wanted to, because he worked in a different time zone from the rest of us. Even the counselling sessions that were part of the deal that kept him in the job after the Dundee game weren't enough to keep him on time. He'd still be sitting around in his training gear at the club, not showered or changed, when he was due at his weekly meeting. I assume he attended them, albeit late, but he never really spoke about it.

For as long as I'd known him, Steve's style was to keep his thoughts to himself. From what I know, it was surprising how open and frank he was in his own autobiography, *Confessions of a Highland Hero*, released in 2009, but I have a confession of my own to make about Stevie's book – I haven't read it. It might sound strange, given I was among the key characters in parts of it, but I already know the script. I was there, living it every day. It doesn't take a book to remind me.

In saying that, Michele has read the book and pointed out a few passages that she thought would interest me. There's nothing that surprised me as such, although the extent of the problems he had at that time do appear to put a lot of things into perspective. I knew things were bad for him away from work while we were at Aberdeen, but I don't think I or any of the staff realised how bad and how low he had sunk at times during that turbulent period.

And the fact is that while he was fighting his demons I had my own turmoil going on. I was there in what should have been my dream job, but all the time hoping for an escape route. The Dundee incident had changed everything for me and I had basically decided that I had to get away from Steve for my own good. I was hoping against hope that somebody would come and offer me a job – a young and ambitious manager with the type of focus and drive that Stevie obviously had when he first went into coaching. Sadly he lost that as other things took over.

The problem for me was that I couldn't actively look for a new job and it isn't the type of profession where you can pick up a paper and apply for a vacancy in the recruitment section. It's all about the old friends network and I don't think anyone on the outside would have thought there was any way I would quit Pittodrie for a new challenge.

Instead I had to sit it out, with the big clock still ticking away over our heads. Really, it was amazing that we got another full season before the axe finally fell, because the writing had been on the wall for months.

25

BEGINNING OF THE END

The problems we had experienced with Steve's drinking at the end of the 2002/03 season left us wide open to being leant on by the club further down the line. Because he had been given a second chance after that ill-fated Dundee game, it was almost as if we owed the club. Soon enough we found out exactly how much it would cost us.

After a year or so in the job we were asked to take a pay cut. I say we were asked, but in reality we were told. In that situation you have two choices: take the pay cut or walk away. Unless you have another job to go to, it would be a fool who chose the latter. David Johnston, the general manager, pulled us in and informed us that we'd need to take a thirteen per cent cut.

It was hard to take because it felt as though we'd been taken to Aberdeen on false pretences. It was as if they'd offered us the big money to get us to agree and then once we were hooked they could go back on everything that had been promised. In fact, the same thing had happened with Ebbe Skovdahl after his honeymoon period was over. There can't be too many professions in the world where an employer can turn round and reduce your pay like that, and leave you looking like the bad guy if you make a fuss. We were all too aware that if we tried to fight the pay cut, it would be turned round to make us look greedy – and that would have been a big own goal in terms of the reaction from the supporters and our reputation within the game. It was a pill we had to swallow, even if it felt like a pretty underhand tactic for the club to use.

It was still a transitional period for us. A lot of young players were tried in the 2003/04 season as we tried to find the right blend. Some, like Scott Morrison, really made an impact, while a succession – including the likes of Richard Buckley, Murray McCulloch, David Donald and John Stewart – flitted in and out of the squad. Young Andrew Considine also made his debut.

We knew we needed experience too, and when Scott Booth became available after a good spell playing his football on the continent it was an easy decision to make. I obviously knew Scott well from our time playing together at Pittodrie and to have a player of his calibre in the squad was a real boost.

We also took Bryan Prunty in from Celtic and had high hopes that he would develop into the finished article. We never got the time to work with him and make the most of the potential we had seen.

Results in that 2003/04 season were horribly inconsistent and incredibly frustrating. We went from the sublime to the ridiculous. The high points included the 2–1 win at Celtic – when Bryan Prunty and David Zdrilic scored – and the 3–0 victory against Dundee United at Pittodrie, when we were three up before half-time. The humiliations included being beaten 4–0 at Kilmarnock and 3–0 by Motherwell at home. All of that left us sitting eleventh when the season finished, with an eight-point cushion over Partick Thistle and thankfully safe from relegation, with a few games to spare.

Although it was a disappointing campaign, Stewart Milne and Keith Wyness were supportive. With a couple of weeks left of the season, Steve came to me and said he was getting another crack at the whip for the following term and that he'd had a good conversation with the chairman about the funds that would be available to bring players in over the summer.

Within a week of the last game, I got a call from someone in the media to tell me that Willie Miller was coming back to the club in some capacity and that his plans didn't involve Steve Paterson or the rest of the management team. It didn't tally with what Steve had told me from his talks with the chairman – but I'd been around long enough to know that rumours usually have some substance.

Sure enough, less than a fortnight after the last day of the 2003/04 season we were called in to Pittodrie. We were sitting in Steve's office when the phone rang and he was told to go through to meet Keith Wyness. I waited until Steve had left the room and turned to Oshor and said: 'You better start packing your bags, that's us on our way.' He thought I was joking but I told him that I was deadly serious. I said: 'Stewart Milne has made his money by working hard – there's no way he's going to sit back and pay someone a good salary to manage this club unless that man is working just as hard as he has had to.'

By that time the club had also found out that Steve had been away on fictitious scouting trips, saying he was going to England to watch matches when really he was away seeing friends in Manchester. Oshor knew and I knew that the only people away every night of the week watching players and opposition teams were the two of us. Steve just didn't bother.

Fifteen minutes after Steve had left the office, the door swung open and he came back in. He looked at the two of us, put his fingers to his head as if he was holding a gun and pretended to pull the trigger. Then he told me that Keith wanted to see me.

Keith and Stewart Milne were waiting for me and I knew what was coming. Stewart told me that of the three of us, sacking me was the hardest one of all. I believed him and said: 'I've enjoyed working with you. Don't feel bad about this. There's only one doorstep that you can lay the blame at and the person's not in this room.' Keith was apologetic, telling me that I'd get full compensation. I honestly didn't even know what was in my contract in that respect and couldn't have cared less about the money. I was gaining a cheque but losing a job that meant the world to me.

Both Keith and Stewart were worried that it would sour what had been a good relationship between the three of us and between me and the club in general. As I told them, I would never say a bad word against Aberdeen Football Club. I may express an opinion about the team from time to time, but I will never have anything but praise for the club as an institution. Nothing they could say or do would turn me against the Dons.

I didn't feel any malice towards the chairman or chief executive. As far as I was concerned, they would have been well within their rights to have sacked Steve after he missed the Dundee game. The decision had come later than I expected, but in my mind it was the right one. You can't have a manager so fragile in his own life trying to look after a group of players and the rest of the staff. The manager has a lot of people's jobs in his hands and has to be in the right frame of mind. It was obvious for Keith and Stewart that their manager was becoming a liability.

The only person I felt any anger towards was Steve himself. I've had a few scraps on football fields in my time but I've never been a street fighter. That day, walking back towards the manager's office, I was about to break the habit of a lifetime. All that was running through my mind was that I was going to teach Steve a lesson – I was ready to chin him. Fortunately I managed to keep myself in check and calmed myself down before I could do anything rash.

Oshor was next to be called through, leaving Steve and me alone. He kept mumbling about Stewart Milne promising to give him more time but I didn't take him on. I knew I'd only say something I'd regret. All the time I was thinking: 'You turn up late for training, never go to watch games and were too drunk to make it to a game. And still it's someone else's fault.'

I don't remember ever really arguing with Steve. We certainly never shouted and swore at each other. I'd always seen him as a loveable rogue and thought I could get him on the straight and narrow. The difference this time was that the Aberdeen job meant more to me than any other – and it was one I knew he could do better than anyone if he only had his mind in the right place.

He was a great football thinker and his ideas were as good as any I've come across in the game. Unfortunately everything combined to make it impossible for him to make a go of it – the drink, the gambling and the pressure of being Aberdeen manager. You shouldn't underestimate how much strain a job like that can put on a man. Some managers go thin, some go fat, some go grey, some go white – all of those things are as a result of the immense pressure they are under. There is a big wage packet every month for managers at the highest level, but there is some penance to pay for that. It is a twenty-four-hour-a-day, seven-day-a-week job. The phone can ring at any time, whether it's the chairman or the press wanting to talk, and you have to be prepared for that. Steve wasn't and he got caught out a couple of times when he wasn't totally sober. He also let his mouth run away a few times in bars while speaking to supporters and before he knew it his comments ended up on websites for all the world to see. It was a shame because he's a genuine character who always likes to tell it like it is. Unfortunately, he found out to his cost that there was no time when he was off duty.

He couldn't see that he had cost us all our jobs and the best opportunity we were ever likely to get in football management. Oshor came back after being told he had been sacked and that was it, over in a flash. I shook both of their hands and walked out to be greeted by the reporters waiting outside. I told them what I'd told the chairman – that the right decision had been made for the good of the club.

It wasn't until later that I discovered Steve had left Pittodrie in the boot of a car. Obviously he thought he was getting the better of the press by doing that but really he played straight into their hands. It was heaven for the headline writers and was a sad way to end it. He should have been brave enough to face up to the press and walk away with his head held high.

Really that decision was typical of his mindset at that moment in time. Whether it was a cloud of drink that was causing it or a form of depression, he was in a bad place. As I mentioned, I haven't read Steve's autobiography, but my wife has read it and has told me about certain passages. Through that I've begun to understand how serious Steve's problems were during that period and I'm glad that we never came to blows on the day we were sacked. In hindsight, I can see it would have been kicking a man when he was down.

Since the day we parted company with Aberdeen, I've spoken to Steve a handful of times. We have never fallen out but we have also never been on the phone every night for a blether. In fact, he'd often get me to phone this manager or that club because he just didn't fancy making the call. I remember having to go behind his back to Keith Wyness when he passed up the chance to join the rest of the SPL managers for a get-together. It was the one and only time I had gone to Keith in that way. I felt it would be a great chance for him to build contacts with the likes of Walter Smith and the other top coaches, the type of networking that can be priceless further down the line. Keith managed to persuade him to go and it proved to be a useful exercise for him. Only Steve can say if he felt he belonged in that type of company, but I know he was every bit as good a manager as any of the household names I worked under during my playing career. Sometimes I wondered if he realised how much potential he had.

It wasn't just other managers Steve could be uncomfortable dealing with. He hated dealing with the press, not least because at Aberdeen it was a daily duty and there was no escaping the media spotlight. It was made worse because there was a paranoia at Pittodrie about the way the club was represented in the press. David Johnston would go through reports with a fine-toothed comb and would often say, 'I don't know why you said that' or, 'Why didn't you try and spin it this way?'. Bearing in mind that this was a man who never spoke to the press, it was difficult to take. It's one thing thinking of strategies to deal with the press, but when you're put on the spot it isn't always the easiest position to be in. At Caley Thistle there hadn't been the same scrutiny and it took a lot of getting used to.

With that added to the pressure, I can understand why it all came to a head for Steve with Aberdeen. I don't hold a grudge and I still class him as a friend. Every now and again he'll call me or I'll pick up the phone for chat with him. Whenever I meet mutual acquaintances, Steve's the first person I ask after and I'm delighted when I hear he's keeping well.

Despite everything we went through, I would actually be happy to work with him in the future. People may think that Steve's had his chance, but in football you never know what is round the next corner or who will be on the end of the line when the phone rings. Steve Paterson remains a big hero in the Highlands and undoubtedly the admiration extends beyond the terraces and into boardrooms in the north of Scotland. I still maintain he is far too good a manager to be out of the game, but if we did ever get the chance to work together again I'd be far firmer with him. I've certainly learnt from the mistakes I made in not getting a tighter grip of him when things started to go off the rails and I paid the price for not doing that when we had our chance at Pittodrie.

26

JOB-SEEKING

When you have spent most of your adult life in professional football, interviews and questions become second nature. I always tried to take the interrogation from the press in my stride and think I gave as good as I got. The first interview I had after being sacked by Aberdeen threw me a bit, and it wasn't a hard-nosed journalist who knocked me off my stride. It was the woman behind the counter at the Job Centre.

After being given my P45 at Pittodrie I took a bit of time off to regroup and reflect on what had happened. Before getting the bad news from the club, we had already booked a summer holiday for the whole family. We went ahead with that Caribbean cruise in the weeks after I cleared my desk and when we came back to Aberdeen I took a few weeks to contemplate my next move.

I found myself out of work for the first time since joining Chelsea as a full-time player, almost twenty-one years earlier. So I did what I thought any man with a wife and two children to support would do and got myself down to the Job Centre.

It had been a long time since I'd been in one of those places but it didn't faze me. I needed a job and it was the obvious place to start looking. The woman who interviewed me was perfectly pleasant and obviously didn't have a clue who I was, which was really neither here nor there.

She took me through the various questions that she had to ask, right through from my name and age to my qualifications. That was when it began to get interesting as I listed my football coaching qualifications. Then she asked what my last job had been. I said: 'Assistant manager of Aberdeen Football Club.' She looked up from her computer screen, only remarking: 'I see.' Then she asked what my last salary had been – and just about fell off her seat when I told her. I suppose I wasn't the normal Job Centre client but I was there for genuine reasons.

She typed in all the information I'd given her and began to run a search. I told her I really didn't think there would be anything in the same line of work for me, that I'd be happy to look at other industries, but she was adamant there would be something out there for me. It was like the *Little Britain* sketch – I was waiting for her to turn round and tell me, 'Computer says no.'

But she didn't. Instead she hit the jackpot. Or at least that's what her computer told her she'd hit. What had come up on the screen was a job that fitted me perfectly, according to my qualifications and experience. It was coaching football for one of the local authorities in London and it carried a salary of £12,000. After giving it all of a second's thought, we agreed that perhaps it wasn't the type of package that would tempt me to uproot my family and start calling round estate agents in London to search me out a new country pile. As I explained to her, in football the jobs don't tend to be advertised in the back of a newspaper and you get used to the old boys' network clicking into place. Everyone knows the way it works and just accepts it. When you're hot property, the offers flow thick and fast and when its someone else's turn you have to take your place at the back of the line.

I was well aware that until the phone rang with an offer from inside the game, I'd have to broaden my horizons to keep a wage coming in. Michele still had a job she loved – working part-time with AVC Media after accepting an invitation from Lesley Little to join the company – but I needed something to keep me occupied.

By the time I made the visit to the Job Centre, I was already going down the path of setting up my own business and that little venture into the city centre had persuaded me that self-employment would be the best way forward because there didn't seem to be much out there for a forty-two-year-old who had known virtually nothing other than football.

By then we were living out at Westhill and I'd struck up a great friendship with our neighbour Jeff Riley, who proved a great support in helping to get my business off the ground. A few months earlier I'd got talking to a driver working for Pinnacle, who ran a fleet of chauffer-driven cars, and it struck me that it was an avenue I could go down.

After weighing everything up and talking to the bank manager, we decided to take the plunge and invest in a top-of-the-range Chrysler Voyager. In business terms the start-up costs were relatively modest and the idea was to launch with the one car while we built contacts, to try and grow the company steadily. It worked well and before long there was regular work, particularly from many of the oil companies.

We had our website up and running and distributed brochures to drum up custom. It helped that people recognised my name and knew my face. Among the clients were a lot of Aberdeen supporters who were keen to listen to tales from my playing days. Golf outings were popular and I'd run people to places like Gleneagles for outings, quite often getting the chance to play myself if there were spaces available. It was a comfortable job and a business with potential, but before long our life took a different direction completely.

We had spent a weekend up in Inverness staying with friends and had a really great time. I watched our son, William, playing football with his pals in the park and it reminded me how happy we had all been living in Inverness before I'd accepted the coaching job at Aberdeen. Eventually I had to call him in and tell him it was time to get in the car and go home, just as we had to do with our daughter Hayley.

William was around fourteen by then and Hayley nearly seventeen. Although both had settled at Hazlehead Academy after we had moved back, it wasn't ideal for them living out at Westhill. We had a lovely house in a quiet cul-de-sac but it was probably too quiet for two teenagers. There wasn't a lot for either of them to do and, because they were at school in Aberdeen rather than Westhill, catching up with friends meant us running them into town and back.

After that weekend in Inverness, all of a sudden it had gone very quiet in the back of the car and I swear I could see a tear in William's eye as we left the old place behind. Eventually I asked what was bothering him and he said what the rest of us already knew: he wanted us to move back to Inverness. We had a few hours to talk things through during the journey back to Aberdeen and by the end of that drive we had more or less made up our minds that the time was right to move on.

Although I thought the business had potential, I was far more interested in making sure we were happy and settled. Hayley was just as keen as William to get back to Inverness and Michele felt it was the right thing for us to do.

Michele had taken my sacking far harder than I had in many ways. When the decision was made by the club, she felt her world was crumbling around her. When something as major as that happens, it's easy for a sense of panic to set in. She was worried that we would lose everything that we had worked so hard for over the years, when in reality that was never going to happen. At that moment, when the rug has just been pulled from under you, it isn't easy to see a rosy future.

Because of that, I could see hatred in Michele's eyes whenever Steve Paterson's name cropped up. It was a shame that it had come to that – but I would imagine Steve could sympathise with that. I'm sure Oshor Williams' wife felt exactly the same way towards him for not making a go of it. Towards the end it was almost as though he was happy to wait for the inevitable and collect his pay-off.

The other side of the coin is that none of us would have ever had that chance with Aberdeen had it not been for Steve's brilliance as a manager in the first place. He had earned the chance by doing the hard work, starting way back in the Highland League with Elgin and Huntly before carrying it on and taking it to a new level with Caley Thistle. I will always be grateful to him for giving me the opportunity to coach Aberdeen and taking me with him to Pittodrie.

In the aftermath of our sacking it was raw for all of us who suffered, but before long that eased and we were able to move on with our lives and start building for the future. Going back to Inverness was part of the process, and a fresh start back where we'd had so many happy times as a family. We sold the house in Westhill, closed down the business without taking a big hit financially and made the move in 2005.

I was fortunate to land a driving job with AJG Parcels in Inverness and the managing director, Adrian Gray, has been fantastically flexible with my commitments in football since then. I'm working with a great group of people and feel like the balance between work, football and family is as good as it has ever been.

Moving back to Inverness was very much a lifestyle choice for us. It was done knowing fine well that in the Highlands the opportunities for me to get back into football full-time would be limited. As I've explained before, that is not the be all and end all for me now.

For two or three months after leaving Pittodrie, I admit I waited for the mobile to ring, hoping for the big offer to get back into the game at the top level. Now I'm too busy to be waiting by the phone and when it does I'll have a big decision to make. At any other stage in my life I made decisions at the drop of a hat. Wherever the best opportunity was I'd go. If that meant moving from Lochaber to London, Chelsea to Yorkshire, Huddersfield to Wiltshire, Swindon to Blackburn, Lancashire to Aberdeen or the north-east to Inverness then I did it. All in all the family moved eleven times following my football career and it got to the stage where we needed stability and to put down roots, without the spectre of having to up sticks again a couple of years down the line. I've kept in touch with some close friends in football and obviously the prospect of teaming up in the future is a subject that has cropped up in conversation. I would never say never, but it would take a very good job to take me away from the life I have now.

We're back in a part of the world I know and love, not a million miles from my old stomping ground on the west coast and just a short drive from Caol when I feel like getting back there to see friends and family. The countryside's on my doorstep and I'm fortunate to have the time to indulge in my passion for fishing and the outdoors.

I have my day job with AJG, I keep in touch with football through work as a youth coach in Inverness – as well as by covering Caley Thistle and Ross County games with the Press Association – and I have time to watch my kids grow up.

Hayley has returned from Edinburgh after training in beauty therapy and William is in his last year at school. I would like to think we've been supportive without being pushy, happy to let each of them make their own choices in the way that we were allowed to as youngsters. Michele and I are looking forward to seeing what the future holds for them and I hope they both know how proud we are of them.

27

TWO JAGS

Since leaving Aberdeen in 2004, my football career has been a tale of two Jags, first with Buckie Thistle and more recently with Caley Thistle. Both have been hugely enjoyable roles with different challenges and I've discovered that I'm still learning about the game all the time.

I had a six-month sabbatical between leaving Pittodrie in May 2004 and being appointed manager of Buckie in October that year. In that time there were a few opportunities to jump back in, but none that really grabbed me and made me think that I had to pursue them.

The job with Thistle was different. From my first meeting with the president Mark Duncan I had a good feeling about the club and when they offered me the chance to take charge of their team in my own right it was too good to turn down. I had a great relationship with Mark in the three and a half years we spent working together and there was nobody more delighted than me in 2010 when the club finally won the Highland League title it had been chasing for more than half a century.

I gave it my best shot to deliver the championship for Mark and the supporters but fell just short, coming close in the league and winning three trophies in four cup final appearances during my time at Victoria Park.

The offer from Buckie came out of the blue. I was invited to talks with Mark and Ian Clark, a director who invested heavily in the club. By the end of that meeting they told me that they were keen to give me the job and asked how I would feel about taking in Graeme McBeath as my assistant. It turned out that they had lined up Graeme for the manager's job but obviously had a change of heart and decided to sound me out.

I knew Graeme vaguely but our paths couldn't have crossed more than once or twice before then. I had absolutely no qualms about agreeing to work with him and I'm glad that I did because it turned out to be an excellent partnership. Graeme had worked wonders with Rothes and because I'd been away from the Highland League for so long, it was important to me to have someone alongside who had a good knowledge of north football.

It was suggested to me that Graeme would come in with the idea of learning from me and then, when the chance for me to move back to full-time football came up, he would step up to take the manager's job. I hope he did benefit from working with me and I know that I certainly learnt from him in that time. We've remained in touch since I left Buckie and I still speak to Graeme once a week to catch up with him.

It was a steep learning curve for me as I adapted to life at that level. The first thing that struck me was the amount of money swilling around in the Highland League and the demands made by players surprised me. To Mark's credit, I was never once refused anything and was in a position to go out and make offers for any player that I wanted.

The dilemma that I had was that I'd sit down to talk terms with this player or that player and find them asking for more and more. I'd be there thinking 'Pal, you're not worth that much.' Unfortunately, because there's a limited pool of players to pick from, clubs have got into the position of paying over the odds in wages and signing-on fees and it has become a vicious circle.

When you have semi-professional players, who by definition have not been good enough to make a career in the full-time game, earning £250 a week, then there's something going wrong. That's before you factor in thousands of pounds in signing-on fees, giving them the type of take-home package that quite a few young full-time players could only dream of. It seemed a bit back to front to me and I got so frustrated I contemplated a playing comeback.

Having trained with the lads, I decided in one game at Inverurie Locos to make an appearance from the bench. We were drawing 1–1 and needed a goal from somewhere, so I stripped off the tracksuit and threw myself on. It was a romantic idea that I could suddenly make a dramatic comeback, but it didn't happen for me. When I'd joined Buckie I'd been asked if I would consider myself for selection and it was an emphatic 'no' as far as I was concerned. Eventually curiosity got the better of me and I had to give it a go. After that one cameo I decided it was time to call it a day once and for all. I didn't want to be hauling myself around the park, well into my forties, and have opposition supporters giving me stick. It was time to be sensible and look for more permanent solutions to fill the spaces in the squad, even if deep down I felt I could still be a useful body to throw on in certain games.

Money wasn't an object for me as I tried to build a team at Buckie, but geography was. Up against teams like Inverurie Locos and Cove Rangers, it was difficult to persuade players based in Aberdeen that they should join us and commit to far more travelling for training and games than they had been used to. There were two or three good players that I went after but I simply couldn't persuade them to make the move out of their comfort zone.

I do fear that one day the chickens will come home to roost for a number of clubs who are just throwing money away every week. Buckie have a steady pair of hands at the tiller in Mark Duncan, a teetotaller who steers clear of the drinking culture that envelops the Highland League, from players through to directors. I've never seen him with anything stronger than a Lucozade and Mark always has his eye on the ball. Logic dictates that the other clubs cannot all go on throwing money at their teams without something having to give.

As I discovered, money is no guarantee of getting the right players in and getting established men to move proved tough. Fortunately I found it easier to recruit more hungry young players and went back to Inverness to take in David Macrae, Craig MacMillan and Lewis MacKinnon. They had been apprentices at Caley Thistle when I was there and I knew all three well enough to be confident that they would strengthen our squad.

Over time we settled into a pattern of play that suited the squad we had and the results were good. In the 2004/05 season, after arriving midway through the campaign, we finished fifth in the league and the following season we were third in the table. In 2006/07 we were challenging for the title before having to settle for third again, so the 2007/08 season was always going to be a make-or-break one. Crucially we lost 2–1 to Cove Rangers with four games to play at the end of that campaign and the chances of winning the Highland League all but disappeared. In the end we missed out by a point. That was the line between success and failure in a season in which we won both the Aberdeenshire Cup and Aberdeenshire Shield. We'd also won the Aberdeenshire Cup in 2005, but it was the championship that was the big prize everyone wanted.

I was beginning to hear whispers that some of the committee were not behind me and that questions were being asked about who was making the decisions when it came to the team. I went to Mark Duncan to tell him what I'd heard and he promised to sort it out. While Mark and his brother Murray were a joy to work with, there were one or two others who helped run the club that I simply couldn't see eye to eye with.

Eventually it came to a head and on the day after the defeat against Cove I was called to a meeting with Mark and told that the club was letting me go. As I said at the time, when you've been sacked by Aberdeen it toughens you to anything else that can be thrown at you. Getting dismissed by Buckie didn't really come close, but I was still disappointed not to have been given the chance to see through what we had started.

More importantly, I was gutted that Graeme McBeath didn't get the chance to step up and take charge of the team. That had been the long-term plan when I joined the club, but in between everything had changed. Mark assured me that Graeme would at least be given the chance to be interviewed for the vacancy, but in actual fact he was only asked to take the boys for the next game and that was that.

Our chances of success were hindered by the training regime we had to approach to cope with the geographical split of the squad. After my move to live back in Inverness, it made sense for me to train the Buckie-based contingent along with the three boys from Inverness. That left Graeme to concentrate on those who stayed in and around Aberdeen, where he was based.

On paper it looked like a brilliant compromise to take into account the split between the two areas, but in practice it was a struggle. Senior clubs like Elgin have tried a similar divide between their central belt and north groups, with limited success. It falls down because unless a squad is working together as one unit there's little chance to work on set pieces or shape. We had to maintain an Aberdeen camp, though, because it was difficult to see the benefit in dragging players who had finished their day job at 5.30pm in Aberdeen on a ninety-minute trek up to Buckie to train on a winter's night.

Despite the challenges, we made the best of the situation and

I really enjoyed being a manager. I had to get used to delivering the team talk, having always had a back seat before, but adopted a very similar style to Steve Paterson. I would say my piece and then step aside to let Graeme say a few words, making sure that if I'd missed anything he had the chance to get the point across. Steve used to do exactly the same with me at Inverness and Aberdeen.

We took Buckie as close to the championship as they had been in many years, but just fell at the final hurdle in our last season. Thankfully they won the league in 2010 and rewarded the supporters for their loyalty, with many of the fans around long enough to see the league change beyond all recognition.

From what I saw at Buckie, the standard in the Highland League has slipped from the level I experienced as a player in the early 1980s. When you consider Inverness Caley, Inverness Thistle, Ross County, Elgin and Peterhead have all been taken out of the set-up to play in the Scottish Football League, it is hardly surprising that the product has been weakened. I don't think any division in the world could cope with losing five of its best sides.

The Highland League's loss has been Caley Thistle and Ross County's gain, with the best young players from across the north drawn to the clubs that can provide senior football on their doorstep.

In 2008 I accepted an invitation to return to the Caley Thistle coaching team as part of the youth development programme, which was led by Danny McDonald at that point. I'd played in the same Clach team as Danny as a youngster and had watched as he built up a formidable record as a coach. Although we knew one another well, Danny was reluctant to approach me and it was left to Charlie Christie to come calling. I think there was an element of fear that I would see myself as overqualified for the role they were suggesting. In truth that isn't a concern that would ever have crossed my mind. I've always been open to anything that sparks my enthusiasm and it was an opportunity that grabbed my attention.

I was asked to help with the club's youth teams, having worked with both the under-seventeens and more recently the under-fifteens, and without hesitation said yes. We train three nights a week and play at weekends, so the time commitment is greater than I had when I was with Buckie. The reward for that is that we are working with a group of eager youngsters who are desperate to learn and to do well in the game. If we can help them on the road then it will all be worthwhile.

We have excellent facilities to work with and the training base for the youth academy at Millburn Academy is a brilliant facility, far ahead of what is being used by many of the other SPL teams. Our pitches, at Charleston Academy, are also perfectly set out and put plenty of teams to shame. As a coach, it's a pleasure to have facilities to match our ambitions for the players under our wing.

The real sense of achievement will come when the young players we are coaching make it through the ranks and into the first team. I spend a lot of time with the strikers, passing on the tricks of the trade, and one day we will hopefully have a good home-grown goal-scorer banging them in for Caley Thistle in the SPL. Martin Bell, my fellow under-fifteen coach, and I see plenty of potential in the teenagers we're working with.

That potential is mirrored throughout the club, where there's a real feel-good factor. Fortunately the ambitions at Inverness are realistic and we are all working towards the goal of establishing the club in the SPL after promotion from the First Division in 2010 – with, hopefully, a good crop of home-grown players waiting in the wings for their chance.

28

THE FINAL CHAPTER

How did a little lad from Lochaber end up travelling the world and rubbing shoulders with some of the biggest names in world football? It's a question I've asked myself plenty of times and I hope the answer is through hard work and determination as well as ability. From those early days striking a ball for hours on end in Caol, everything I've achieved in life has been by making my own luck.

There have been plenty of highs along the way and I've lived a life of very few regrets. I can look back on a career that is beyond any of the dreams I harboured when I was a young man trying to make my way in the world. I started out not even knowing whether I'd get a chance at the top level and ended up savouring some of the most momentous occasions any professional could hope for.

I've played in cup finals, scored for my country, worked with World Cup winners and national heroes, performed at some of the most iconic stadiums in the game and won trophies along the way.

Picking a highlight from nearly twenty years as a player is difficult, but there is one moment in time that sticks in my mind and not surprisingly it involved hitting the back of the net. Asking a striker to pick their favourite goal is like asking a dad to choose between his children, yet it is a question I've often been asked.

I could reel off a list of my favourites: most spectacular, best header, hardest hit, most celebrated . . . the categories are endless. There was one goal in particular that combined a few of those factors and it came on 6 May 1995 at Pittodrie. Dundee United were the opposition and it was a game that both teams needed to win to try and claw clear of the relegation place. Billy Dodds gave us the lead but the game was still on a knife-edge when wee Billy went scampering away down the left wing on a quick break. I was charging forward to support him and he squared the ball perfectly across the eighteen-yard line into my path. It was down to me and the United keeper Kieran O'Hanlon then and as soon as the shot left my right boot I knew there was only going to be one winner. It was as clean a strike as you could wish for and the ball flew past the keeper low at his left corner. To make it perfect, it was right in front of the Richard Donald Stand. Both tiers were absolutely bouncing when that goal went in – they knew and I knew how important it could be. Robbie Winters pulled a goal back for United later in the match but we came through to win 2–1 and the following week it was Dundee United who dropped down to the First Division.

I was fortunate enough to score the decisive goal in a cup final for Aberdeen – but I would say survival in the Premier Division was far more important to the club than lifting silverware. Because of that, the goal against Dundee United ranks as probably the most important of my career and it's the one I treasure above all of the rest.

Surprisingly, the most memorable match of my life is one that I didn't score in. The play-off final for Swindon, when we beat Sunderland in 1990 to win promotion to the First Division, was an unforgettable experience. I couldn't begin to count the number of times I'd passed Wembley dreaming of one day playing there. With Chelsea we trained at Stamford Bridge every Friday and I'd catch the train in from Amersham to Baker Street, changing there for Fulham Broadway. During that journey to Baker Street the tube would pass Wembley and even the name was enough to send a tingle down my spine. Occasionally we would head into London on a Sunday for the big market held outside Wembley and again I'd be there under the twin towers, daydreaming about what was on the other side.

By the time I got my chance to play there I had never even been inside the famous old ground. Finally getting through the door was an incredible sensation, sitting in the dressing rooms that had been home to so many legendary players and had seen so many dramas played out. To play at Wembley in front of almost 73,000 supporters and to win was fairytale stuff for me. I'd watched the likes of Kenny Dalglish gracing the Wembley pitch; I'd seen the Tartan Army ripping down the goalposts. All of a sudden I was there on *that* pitch, I was living the dream. It was an unforgettable day and the fact that the old stadium has been consigned to the history books makes it all the more special and nostalgic. I feel privileged to have had that opportunity and I'll always cherish that occasion.

Swindon gave me that chance to play at Wembley and also gave me the time I spent working with the greatest manager I ever encountered: Ossie Ardiles. Again, I count myself extremely fortunate to have fallen under the wing of some real legends of the game. From Glenn Hoddle and Kenny Dalglish to Willie Miller, there were some really strong personalities and excellent coaches.

For me, though, Ossie was a class apart. I never heard him shouting and swearing, everything was very cool, composed and collected. He had the ability to relax and inspire players and his mantra was always 'play football, play football, play football'. That was his answer to everything, simple but effective.

When he watched his first training session at Swindon we were being put through our paces by Chic Bates – inherited by

Ossie when Lou Macari moved on to West Ham. We were in a circle doing a little possession exercise when a few of us started to mess around with little flicks and tricks. I've seen it happen a hundred times before and the outcome is always the same, the ball gets put away and the running starts as a punishment. Chic started to go down that road until Ossie intervened: 'play football, play football'. The ball stayed and the runs never happened.

The way Ossie had us playing was a joy to behold. There's a DVD of the season, culminating with promotion at Wembley, called *A Day to Remember*. The title sums it up nicely and we played football to remember. I've nothing but great memories of that period in my life.

The best managers are the ones who can get the best out of their players, regardless of resources or the ability of the squad they have at their disposal. For me and everyone else in that team, there was no doubt that we were desperate to succeed for the man. Not one player would have a bad word to say about him. To have played under Ossie, Glenn, Kenny and the many other excellent coaches and managers I worked with undoubtedly made me a better person.

I also had the joy of playing alongside a long list of wonderful individuals who would not have been out of place in any of the greatest club sides. If I had to pick a team from all those I lined up with through the years, I would have to plump for Jim Leighton as the goalkeeper. Jim was a tremendous all-rounder and in my opinion should have got the nod ahead of Andy Goram for Scotland every time. The fact that Andy and Jim were battling for that one place in the national team made it impossible for anyone else to get a look in, which was bad news for my good friend Nicky Walker. Nicky's talents deserved greater recognition. He was a great shot-stopper and also one of the best kickers of the ball in his position.

At the heart of any defence I don't think you could ask for a better partnership than the two Colins: Calderwood and Hendry.

Colin Calderwood, who I played with at Swindon and for Scotland, is another good friend of mine and I have always admired the way he worked his way up through the ranks from Stranraer to Macclesfield to Swindon and then Tottenham and Scotland. He is one of the hardest-working men in football and deserves every bit of the success he has enjoyed. Colin Hendry, who was a team-mate at Blackburn, struck up a good under-standing with Calderwood and, with my forward's hat on, was the type of defender every striker hated playing against.

At full-back, I'd single out Stewart McKimmie as the best right-back I ever played alongside. Stewart was a real tough nut and would drag people up to his high standards – he hated to see anyone falling below what he expected of them. On the other side of the defence, Paul Bodin at Swindon was a revelation. He came to the club from Newport County but despite those humble beginnings, he was a total footballer. Paul could turn defence into attack, with real pace and attacking flair. He went on to play many times for Wales and was a real class act.

In midfield I'd go for silk over steel, with a combination of Gary McAllister, John Collins, Paul McStay and Gordon Cowans. I'll never forget watching in horror as the Tartan Army booed and jeered Gary during one international. He was a midfielder who proved himself to be out of the very top drawer with Leeds, Coventry and Liverpool – not to mention an incredible captain to the national side. He didn't deserve that type of treatment – and he went on to win over the supporters with his ability and attitude.

Paul McStay was another player who never really became a fans' favourite – he was more of a player's player. He played the game simply but had a great football brain, understated but brilliant at the same time.

John Collins was more of a showman and had as sweet a left foot as I've ever seen. He also had a dedication to fitness like no other man I've ever met. He was meticulous about nutrition and particularly fresh fruit. John's the only person I've known who would peel the skin from a pear before eating it. He'd be busy doing that while John McGinlay and I were tucking into cream buns.

Not many could have matched John for physical prowess, but Gordon Cowans would have been one of them. Gordon had an incredible natural stamina and that was mated to an ability to retain possession in a way that used to make me marvel. Playing alongside Gordon at Blackburn was an absolute pleasure and he must rank as one of the unsung heroes of that successful Rovers side. A real star.

I've never been known as a selfless type of person when it comes to football, so there's no chance I would keep myself out of my dream team to give someone else a place. I'd be there hoping to take the glory. I remember Willie Miller being asked who his best signing was as Aberdeen manager and he mentioned my name in reply, with the caveat that I was a terrible team player. He rightly pointed out that I was more interested in scoring goals than doing my bit for the side. But, as Willie also pointed out, every team needs a player with that single-minded approach to scoring goals. You need that one individual who will go the extra yard to get on the end of a cross or a pass because they are desperate to score. That is what gets teams out of trouble more often than not – I don't buy into this nonsense that it doesn't matter who scores the goals as long as the team is winning. It makes my blood boil when strikers trot out that line because it's just an attempt to mask their own deficiencies or poor form. Any forward worth their salt should be beating themselves up if they leave the pitch without doing what they are paid to do: scoring goals.

Because of that, I'd choose a man with the same outlook as me to make up the front two. Steve White and I both got twenty-seven goals apiece in Swindon's promotion-winning season and that was purely and simply because we were both focused solely on getting into the box and scoring goals.

There was no telepathic understanding or mysterious formula to the way we played. It was just back-to-basics forward play – get in the box and get on the end of every cross and pass that comes your way. Managers can sometimes be guilty of trying to over-complicate that area of their team, searching endlessly for the perfect pairing. In actual fact, if you have two natural goal-scorers leading the line you won't go far wrong.

That would be as close to my dream team as I could get, although there are dozens of other players who I played with over the years who would be knocking on the door. If that is my perfect team, then my perfect job is the one that I once had: coaching at Aberdeen. I feel I have a lot of unfinished business at Pittodrie and I would dearly love to get a second crack at it to make amends for the disappointment of the first time, when we simply never got off the ground.

To go back with a manager with the energy and total focus to make a go of it would be a dream. It's rare in football to get a second chance at anything but then, as one old striker never tired of telling us, 'It's a funny old game'. I'm still the same coach who the Dons were so keen to take to Pittodrie along with Steve Paterson not so long ago. I still have the passion for the game that I have always had, as well as the will to win that became a trademark of my game as a player. I'm still working hard as a coach, learning all the time. In this profession you never know who or what is just around the corner – but my gut feeling is that the final chapter in this story has yet to be written.